Collins

阿加莎·克里斯蒂经典侦探作品集

黑麦奇案
A Pocket Full of Rye

〔英〕阿加莎·克里斯蒂 著

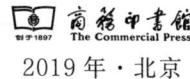

2019年·北京

Agatha Christie

A Pocket Full of Rye

©HarperCollins Publishers Ltd.（2012）

©English-Chinese simplified character rights

The Commercial Press（2019）

怎样开启你的TING笔

 如需使用TING笔，请如图所示长按开/关键2秒直至听到开机音乐。

 用TING笔笔尖点击圆圈中心，你将听到一段音乐提示。这段音乐提示在你每次阅读点击TING书的时候都会出现。

 现在你就可以使用TING笔并体验惊喜啦！

说明：如果你希望购买TING笔的配件、获得最新资讯或寻求帮助，请与我们联系或登录TING的门户网站：http://ting-pen.com

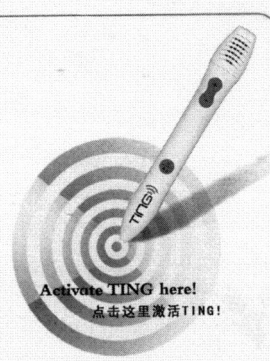

Activate TING here!
点击这里激活TING!

可以了！你的TING笔现在已经准备好了。

出版说明

商务印书馆创立以来，始终以"昌明教育，开启民智"为己任，致力于移译西学、沟通中外，坚持以高质量的出版物促进文化交流，以传播先进思想推动社会进步。近年来更是加大了外语学习读物的出版，如推出了"莎翁戏剧经典"丛书等。此次引进"阿加莎·克里斯蒂经典侦探作品集"系列，是我馆开发英语学习读物的又一成果。

阿加莎·克里斯蒂（Agatha Christie 1890—1976）是英国著名女侦探小说家、剧作家，三大推理文学宗师之一，被誉为举世公认的推理小说女王。其作品已被翻译成一百多种语言，曾多次被搬上银幕。代表作有《东方快车谋杀案》和《尼罗河上的惨案》等，在中国有大批爱好者，读者接受度很高。

这套"阿加莎·克里斯蒂经典侦探作品集"丛书，是英国柯林斯出版公司精选的阿加莎·克里斯蒂的经典作品，由英国语言和文学专家专门为世界各地母语非英语的读者改编设计，每篇小说经过适当删减，其中的词汇和语法也做了简化，是适合中等以上英语水平读者学习的英语读物。

为方便读者使用，中文注释本以脚注的形式给难词标注词性和释义；提供英汉对照的作者简介、出场人物表及文化注释；本书配有全文朗读音频,由英国本土人士录制,声情并茂地再现精彩的故事内容,以点读笔和二维码的形式提供给读者。

希望这套"阿加莎·克里斯蒂经典侦探作品集"丛书,能够帮助读者在欣赏英文小说的同时学习英语、提高英语能力,成为读者英语阅读和学习的最佳选择。

商务印书馆编辑部

2019 年 5 月

目　录

作者简介 ·· 4

人物表 ·· 6

正文 ·· 1

文化注释 ·· 115

作者简介

Agatha Christie

Agatha Christie (1890-1976) is known throughout the world as the Queen of Crime. Her books have sold over a billion copies in English with another billion in over 100 foreign languages. She is the most widely published and translated author of all time and in any language; only the Bible and Shakespeare have sold more copies. She is the author of 80 crime novels and short story collections, 19 plays, and six other novels. *The Mousetrap*, her most famous play, was first staged in 1952 in London and is still performed there—it is the longest-running play in history.

Agatha Christie's first novel was published in 1920. It featured Hercule Poirot, the Belgian detective who has become the most popular detective in crime fiction since Sherlock Holmes.

阿加莎·克里斯蒂

阿加莎·克里斯蒂(1890—1976)在世界各地被誉为"侦探小说女王"。她以英语出版的作品销量超过十亿册,而以一百多种外语出版的作品销量也达到了十亿册。她是迄今为止以各语种得到最广泛出版和译介的作家,其作品销量仅次于《圣经》和莎士比亚的作品。她著有80部侦探题材的长篇小说和短篇小说集、19部剧作及其他6部小说。《捕鼠器》是她最有名的剧作,1952年在伦敦被首次搬上舞台,直到今天还在上演——它也成为历史上演出时间最长的戏剧。

阿加莎·克里斯蒂的第一部小说出版于1920年,其中塑造了比利时大侦探赫尔克里·波洛这一人物——他已成为自夏洛克·福尔摩斯以来犯罪小说里最知名的侦探。柯林斯出版公司自1926年至今一直在出版阿加莎·克里斯蒂的作品。

人 物 表

Somers 小姐：联合信托公司（Consolidated Investments Trust，简称 CIT）的打字员

Griffith 小姐：联合信托公司打字员的主管

Irene Grosvenor 小姐：联合信托公司所有人 Rex Fortescue 的私人秘书

Rex Fortescue 先生：拥有联合信托公司的富商

Isaacs 医生：在联合信托公司附近工作的医生

Edwin Sandeman 爵士：Rex Fortescue 的私人医生

Neele 督察：苏格兰场警官

Hay 探长：Neele 督察的下属

Bernsdorff 医生：圣犹大医院（St Jude's Hospital）的医生

Adele Fortescue 夫人：Rex Fortescue 的第二任妻子

Elaine Fortescue 小姐：Rex Fortescue 和第一任妻子的女儿

Percival Fortescue 先生：Rex Fortescue 的长子

Lance Fortescue 先生：Rex Fortescue 的幼子

Jennifer Fortescue 夫人：Percival Fortescue 的妻子

Patricia（Pat）Fortescue 夫人：Lance Fortescue 的妻子

Crump 先生：Rex Fortescue 的男管家

Mary Dove：Rex Fortescue 的女管家

Crump 夫人：Rex Fortescue 的厨师，与 Crump 先生是夫妻

Gerald Wright：与 Elaine Fortescue 相恋的教师

Gladys Martin：Rex Fortescue 的用餐女侍

Ellen Curtis：Rex Fortescue 的女佣

Effie Ramsbottom 小姐：Rex Fortescue 第一任妻子的姐姐
Vivian Dubois 先生：Adele Fortescue 的朋友
助理警察总监：苏格兰场的高级警官，Neele 的上司
Albert Evans：Gladys Martin 的男朋友
Jane Marple 小姐：善于侦破凶杀案的老妇人
Helen MacKenzie 夫人：Rex Fortescue 曾经的生意伙伴的遗孀
Ansell 先生：为 Adele Fortescue 工作的律师
Billingsley 先生：为 Rex Fortescue 工作的律师
Crosbie 医生：松林私人疗养院（Pinewood Private Sanatorium）的负责人
Donald MacKenzie：Helen MacKenzie 的儿子
Ruby MacKenzie：Helen MacKenzie 的女儿
Kitty：正在接受 Marple 小姐用餐女侍培训的女孩

Agatha Christie

A Pocket Full of Rye

Chapter 1

Miss Somers, who was not the best typist in the office, poured the tea and took the cups round.

Miss Griffith, the well-organized head typist who had been with *Consolidated Investments*① *Trust* for sixteen years, tasted her tea and asked sharply②, 'Are you sure the water was boiling when you put it on the tea leaves, Somers? If it isn't boiling, the tea tastes horrible!'

At that moment Miss Grosvenor, an incredibly glamorous③ blonde, who was Mr Fortescue's personal secretary, came in to make his tea herself. Then she went out again, carrying the tea tray in front of her.

Mr Fortescue's office was a large room with a shining wood floor and behind a huge desk sat Mr Fortescue, a large, fat man with a bald head. Miss Grosvenor put the tray on the desk saying quietly, 'Your tea, Mr Fortescue,' then left. Miss Grosvenor went back into her own office, made two telephone calls and looked at the clock. It was ten minutes past eleven. Just then a terrible cry came from Mr Fortescue's office. Miss Grosvenor rushed in and found her employer behind his desk, his body twisting in pain. He was finding it difficult to speak.

'Tea — what did you put in the tea — get a doctor …'

Miss Grosvenor went running into the typists' office, shouting, 'Mr Fortescue — we must get a doctor — I'm sure he's dying.'

---

① investment *n*. 投资　② sharply *adv.* 尖锐地　③ glamorous *adj.* 特别富有魅力的

But it had never been necessary to call a doctor to the office before now. Where was there a doctor nearby? Miss Griffith said, 'We can call his own doctor! Get the private address book.' Then, just to be sure, she told the office boy to go out and find a doctor — *anywhere*.

Miss Grosvenor said tearfully, 'There couldn't have been anything wrong with the tea. But Mr Fortescue — he said it was the tea...'

A short while later Dr Isaacs, a local doctor the office boy had found and Sir Edwin Sandeman, Mr Fortescue's doctor, met in the lift.

Chapter 2

Detective Inspector① Neele sat behind Mr Fortescue's desk. One of his officers sat quietly against the wall near the door with a notebook. Inspector Neele looked like an ordinary man, but his way of thinking was very imaginative.

Miss Griffith had just left, after giving him an exact report of the morning's events. Inspector Neele thought of possible reasons why the head typist could have poisoned② her employer's tea, and rejected them as unlikely, because Miss Griffith was (*a*) not the type of person to be a poisoner, (*b*) not in love with her employer, (*c*) not a woman who held grudges③.

It was possible, of course, that Mr Fortescue's sudden illness had a natural cause, but neither Dr Isaacs nor Sir Edwin Sandeman had thought so.

Miss Grosvenor now came in and said at once, 'I didn't do it! There wasn't anything wrong with the tea!'

Inspector Neele thought of a possible reason why Miss Grosvenor might have poisoned Mr Fortescue: perhaps a love affair that had gone wrong?

'I see,' said Inspector Neele. 'Your name and address, please?'

'Irene Grosvenor, 14 Rushmoor Road, Muswell Hill.'

No love affair, Neele said to himself. The address was a respectable④ one and she probably lived there with her parents.

---

① Detective Inspector *n*. 督察(参见 115 页**文化注释**) ② poison *v*. 给……下毒 ③ hold a grudge 记仇 ④ respectable *adj*. 正派的

Inspector Neele questioned her about how she had made Mr Fortescue's tea. The cup, saucer① and teapot had already been sent for analysis②. Irene Grosvenor and only Irene Grosvenor had touched that cup, saucer and teapot. The kettle③ had been refilled from the tap in the small kitchen by Miss Grosvenor.

'And the tea itself?' asked Neele.

'It was Mr Fortescue's own special China tea. We keep it in my room.'

Inspector Neele asked about sugar and heard that Mr Fortescue didn't take sugar. The telephone rang and Inspector Neele picked it up and spoke. 'Sergeant④ Hay?' He nodded to Miss Grosvenor and said, 'That's all for now, thank you.' She went out of the room quickly.

'He died five minutes ago, you say?' Neele said into the phone. Sergeant Hay had gone to St Jude's Hospital, where Mr Fortescue had been taken. *Twelve forty-three*, he wrote in his notebook. Hay then said that Dr Bernsdorff would like to speak to Inspector Neele. A moment later a loud voice made Neele take the telephone away from his ear.

'Hello, you old crime hunter!' Inspector Neele and Dr Bernsdorff of St Jude's had worked together on a case⑤ of poisoning a year ago and had become friends.

'Mr Fortescue's dead, I hear, doc. And the cause of death?'

'There will have to be an autopsy⑥, naturally. It's a very interesting case. Very interesting indeed.'

'You don't think it was a natural death?' asked Neele.

'Not a chance of it.'

---

① saucer *n*. 茶碟　② analysis *n*. 化验分析　③ kettle *n*. 水壶
④ Sergeant *n*. 探长(参见 115 页**文化注释**)　⑤ case *n*. 案件　⑥ autopsy
n. 尸检(参见 116 页**文化注释**)

'He was poisoned?'

'Definitely. And I'm almost sure what the poison was. Taxine, my boy. Taxine.'

'Taxine? I've never heard of it,' said Neele.

'It's really very unusual! I don't think I would have thought of it myself if I hadn't had a case only three weeks ago. A couple of kids playing dolls' tea parties pulled some berries① off a yew tree② and made tea with them. *Extremely* poisonous, but I don't think I've heard of a case where it was used deliberately③. It really is *most* interesting and unusual. You've no idea, Neele, how boring it is when weedkiller④ is used all the time. Interesting for you, too, I would think!'

'So enjoyable for everyone, is that the idea? Except for the victim⑤. Did he say anything before he died?'

'He said that he had been given something in his tea at the office — but that's nonsense⑥, because taxine doesn't work that fast. It takes two or three hours to work. And if he had eaten a big breakfast, it would take even longer.'

'Breakfast,' said Inspector Neele thoughtfully. 'Thanks, doctor. I'd like to speak to my Sergeant again, if you don't mind.'

Moments later Sergeant Hay said urgently, '*Sir*. The suit the victim was wearing — I checked the contents of the pockets. There were the usual things — handkerchief, keys, change, wallet — but there was one thing that's really strange. The right-hand pocket of his jacket had grain⑦ in it. It looked like rye⑧ to me. Quite a lot of it.'

---

① berries *n.* 浆果　② yew tree *n.* 紫杉（参见 118 页**文化注释**）　③ deliberately *adv.* 故意地　④ weedkiller *n.* 除草剂　⑤ victim *n.* 受害者　⑥ nonsense *n.* 胡话　⑦ grain *n.* 谷物　⑧ rye *n.* 黑麦

Inspector Neele got up and went into the typists' office. 'Miss Griffith? Can I have a word with you?'

Miss Griffith followed Neele back into Mr Fortescue's office and he said, 'I have heard from St Jude's Hospital. Mr Rex Fortescue died at 12.43.'

'I was afraid he was very ill,' she said.

She was not, Neele noted, at all upset. 'Will you please give me the details of his home and family?'

'Of course. I tried to speak to Mrs Fortescue, but it seems she is out playing golf. They do not know where she is playing, but they will tell her that Mr Fortescue is in hospital when she returns. I've written down the telephone number for you, but they live at Baydon Heath and the name of the house is Yewtree Lodge ...'

'*What?*' exclaimed Neele, immediately connecting the name of the house with the poison that had been used.

Miss Griffith looked at him with interest, but Inspector Neele said no more on the subject. 'Can you give me details of his family?'

'Mrs Adele Fortescue is his second wife. She is much younger than he is. The first Mrs Fortescue has been dead a long time. There are two sons and a daughter from the first marriage. The daughter, Elaine, lives at home and so does the elder son, Percival, who is a partner in the firm[①]. He is away in the north of England today on business. They are expecting him to return tomorrow.'

'When did he go away?'

'The day before yesterday.'

'And the second son?'

---

① firm *n*. 公司

'Because of a disagreement with his father, Lance Fortescue lives abroad.'

'Are both sons married?'

'Yes. Mr Percival has been married for three years. He and his wife, Jennifer, are moving into their own house soon.'

'You were not able to get in touch with Jennifer Fortescue either, when you rang?'

'She had gone to London for the day.' Miss Griffith went on, 'Mr Lance got married less than a year ago. To the widow① of Lord Frederick Anstice. I expect you've seen pictures of Mrs Patricia in magazines such as the Tatler② — with horses, you know. And at horse races③.'

Neele assumed that the disagreement with his father was because young Lance Fortescue had been guilty④ of some bad behaviour, possibly in business. And now he was married to the widow of Lord Frederick Anstice, a man who had killed himself rather than face an inquiry⑤ about his racehorses.

Neele picked up the phone and dialled and soon a man's voice said, 'Baydon Heath 3400.'

'I want to speak to Mrs Adele Fortescue or Miss Elaine Fortescue.'

'They aren't in, either of them.'

'Are you the butler⑥?'

'That's right.'

'Is there anyone in the house I can speak to about Mr Rex Fortescue's illness?'

'Well, there's Miss Dove, the housekeeper.'

---

① widow *n*. 遗孀 ② Tatler *n*.《尚流》杂志(一本评论富有、时尚人士生活和各类活动的杂志) ③ horse race *n*. 赛马 ④ guilty *adj*. 有罪的 ⑤ inquiry *n*. 调查 ⑥ butler *n*. 男管家

'I'll speak to Miss Dove, please.'

A minute or two later a woman's voice spoke. 'This is Miss Dove.' The voice was low and musical.

'I am sorry to have to tell you, Miss Dove, that Mr Rex Fortescue died a short time ago. I need to contact his relatives ...'

'Of course,' she said, her voice calm. 'The person you really want to speak to is Mr Percival Fortescue. You might find him at the *Midland Hotel* in Manchester or possibly at the *Grand* in Leicester. Mrs Adele Fortescue will be home for dinner and she may be in to tea. It will be a great shock to her. Mr Fortescue was well when he left here this morning. What was it? His heart?'

'Did he have heart trouble?' Neele asked.

'No, but as it was so sudden ...' She broke off①. 'Are you speaking from St Jude's Hospital?'

'No, Miss Dove, I'm speaking from Mr Fortescue's office. I am Detective Inspector Neele and I will be coming down to see you as soon as I can get there.'

'Detective Inspector? Do you mean ... what *do* you mean?'

'Miss Dove, when there is a sudden death, we are called to the scene②, especially when the deceased③ hadn't seen a doctor lately — he hadn't, had he?'

'No. Mr Percival made an appointment twice for him, but he refused to go. He was quite unreasonable④— they were all worried ...' She broke off and then continued as calmly as before. 'If Mrs Fortescue returns to the house before you arrive, what do you want me to tell her?'

What a practical and sensible woman she is, thought Inspector

---

① break off 停顿 ② scene *n*. 案发现场 ③ deceased *n*. 逝者
④ unreasonable *adj*. 不讲道理的

Neele. Aloud he said, 'Just tell her that in a case of sudden death we have to make a few inquiries. Routine① inquiries.'

---

① routine *adj.* 例行的

Chapter 3

Neele looked at Miss Griffith seriously. 'So they wanted him to see a doctor. You didn't tell me that.'

'I didn't think of it,' said Miss Griffith. 'He never seemed to me really *ill* — just unlike himself. Once or twice I thought he had been drinking ... For most of the time I've been here he was always very secretive about his business affairs①, but recently he'd been talking openly about them, and spending large amounts of money — which wasn't like him. It seemed like he was looking forward to something exciting. And some very strange-looking people came to see him on business. It worried Mr Percival. Mr Fortescue was doing a lot of things that Mr Percival thought were unwise. But suddenly his father didn't listen to him any more and Mr Percival was very upset.'

'And they had a real fight about it all?' Inspector Neele asked.

'I don't know about a *fight*, but once, Mr Fortescue came into the typists' room with Mr Percival and he called him names and swore② at him. He said Mr Percival was too scared to expand the business in a big way. He said, "I shall bring Lance home again. He's worth ten of you — *and* he married well. Lance is fearless③ and brave, even if he did risk a criminal prosecution④ once." Oh dear, I wish I hadn't said that!'

'Don't worry,' said Inspector Neele comfortingly⑤. 'What's past is past. Tell me a little more about the staff here.'

---

① affairs *n*. 事务   ② swear [swore] *v*. 咒骂；发誓   ③ fearless *adj*. 无畏的   ④ criminal prosecution *n*. 刑事检控   ⑤ comfortingly *adv*. 安慰地

Chapter 4

Inspector Neele was looking at the outside of Yewtree Lodge, a large, solid, red-brick building. The gardens were laid out in rose beds and ponds, with large numbers of neat yew hedges① — and there was a huge yew tree, clearly very old. And possibly the poisonous berries from that very tree …? Inspector Neele rang the bell. The door was opened by a nervous-looking middle-aged man who invited Neele and Sergeant Hay in.

'Has Mrs Adele Fortescue returned yet?'

'No, Sir.'

'Nor Miss Elaine Fortescue?'

'No, Sir.'

'Then I would like to see Miss Dove, please.'

The man turned his head slightly. 'Here's Miss Dove now — coming down the stairs.'

The word housekeeper had given Neele an impression of someone large and powerful, dressed in black, and so the Inspector was quite unprepared for the small neat figure coming towards him. The light brown colour of her dress with its white collar② and cuffs③, the neat waves of hair and the slight smile, all seemed a little unreal, as though this young woman of under thirty was playing a part; not, Neele thought, the part of a housekeeper, but the part of Mary Dove, gentle and quiet like the bird, the dove④, that shared her surname.

'Inspector Neele?'

'Yes. This is Sergeant Hay. It seems likely that Mr

---

① hedge *n*. 树篱　② collar *n*. 衣领　③ cuff *n*. 袖口　④ dove *n*. 鸽子

Fortescue's death was caused by something he ate at breakfast this morning. I would like Sergeant Hay to be taken to the kitchen, where he can ask about the food that was served.'

Her eyes met his for a moment, thoughtfully, then she said, 'Of course.' She turned to the butler, who was standing nervously nearby. 'Crump, will you take Sergeant Hay?'

The two men left. Mary Dove said to Neele, 'Will you come in here?' She opened the door of a sitting room and led him into it. 'Please sit down.'

Mary Dove sat opposite him. She chose, he noticed, to face the light. An unusual choice for a woman. Still more unusual if a woman had anything to hide. But perhaps Mary Dove had nothing to hide.

'Mrs Adele Fortescue may return at any minute. And so may Mrs Jennifer. I have sent telegrams① to Mr Percival Fortescue at various places.'

'Thank you, Miss Dove.'

'You say that Mr Fortescue's death was caused by something he may have eaten for breakfast? It seems unlikely. For breakfast this morning there was bacon and eggs, coffee, toast and marmalade. There was a cold ham, too, but that was also eaten yesterday, and no one was ill. No fish of any kind was served. For dinner last night ...'

'No.' Inspector Neele interrupted her. 'We are not interested in dinner last night. Will you tell me exactly what Mr Fortescue ate and drank this morning?'

'He had early tea brought to his room at eight o'clock. Breakfast was at a quarter past nine. Mr Fortescue had eggs, bacon, coffee, toast and marmalade.'

---

① telegram *n*. 电报

'Any cereal①?'

'No, he didn't like cereal.'

'The sugar for the coffee ...'

'Mr Fortescue did not take sugar in his coffee,' Miss Dove interrupted.

'Did he take any medicines in the morning?'

'No, nothing like that.'

'Who was at breakfast?'

'Mrs Adele, Miss Elaine and Mrs Jennifer. Mrs Adele has only coffee, orange juice and toast, Mrs Jennifer and Miss Elaine always eat a large breakfast. As well as eating eggs and cold ham, they would probably have cereal as well. Mrs Jennifer drinks tea, not coffee.'

Three people had had breakfast with the deceased. Any of them might have had the opportunity to put taxine in Fortescue's cup of coffee. The bitterness② of the coffee would have hidden the bitter taste of the taxine ... Neele looked up to find Mary Dove watching him.

'Your questions about medicines seem to me rather strange, Inspector,' she said. 'It seems to suggest that either there was something wrong with a medicine, or that something had been put into it.'

Neele looked at her seriously. 'I did not say that Mr Fortescue died of *food* poisoning. But some kind of poisoning. In fact — just poisoning.'

She repeated quietly, 'Poisoning ...' She appeared neither surprised nor anxious③, simply interested. She said, 'I have never been involved with a poisoning case before.'

'It's not very pleasant,' Neele told her.

---

① cereal *n*. 麦片   ② bitterness *n*. 苦味   ③ anxious *adj*. 焦虑的；渴望的

'No — I suppose not ...' She looked up at him with a sudden smile. 'I didn't do it,' she said. 'But I suppose everybody says that!'

'Have you any idea who *did* do it, Miss Dove?'

She shrugged① her shoulders. 'He was a horrible man. Anybody might have done it.'

'Miss Dove, tell me something about the household② here.'

She looked up at him. He was a little surprised to see she looked amused.

'I don't want what I am going to say to be repeated at the inquest③, but I would like to say it — unofficially.'

'I'm listening, Miss Dove.'

She leaned back. 'Let me start by saying that I've no feeling of loyalty④ to my employers. I work for them because it's a job that pays well and I insist that it pays well.'

Neele said, 'I was a little surprised to find you doing this type of job. With your obvious intelligence ...'

'I ought to be working in an office?' interrupted Mary Dove. 'My dear Inspector Neele, some people will pay anything — *anything* — to avoid household worries. Firstly, finding and employing staff is very boring. Secondly, running the house properly requires abilities that most of the people I work for don't have.'

'And what happens if your staff leave you unexpectedly? I've heard of such things.'

Mary smiled. 'If necessary, I can make the beds, clean the rooms, cook a meal *and* serve it, without anyone noticing the difference. But I work only for the extremely rich, who will

---

① shrug your shoulders 耸肩　② household *n*. 全家人　③ inquest *n*. 死因审理　④ loyalty *n*. 忠诚

pay anything to be comfortable. I pay top prices and so I get the best people available.'

'Such as the butler?' Neele asked, remembering the nervous Crump, whose red nose said he clearly liked alcohol too much.

She was amused. 'Crump stays because of Mrs Crump, who is one of the best cooks I've ever worked with. As for Crump, he's not such a bad butler, really. I keep the key of the wine cellar and I watch the whisky and gin carefully. But you wanted to know what I think of the family. They are all really horrible. The late① Mr Fortescue was the type of businessman who is always careful to work just on the right side of the law. He was rude and a bully②. Mrs Fortescue, Adele — is about thirty years younger than he was — with real sex appeal, if you know what I mean.'

Inspector Neele was shocked. A girl like Mary Dove ought not to say such things, he felt.

The young lady was continuing, 'Adele married him for his money, and Percival and Elaine are as nasty as they can be to her, but she doesn't care. Rex Fortescue would do anything for her. Oh dear, the wrong tense. I haven't really understood yet that he's dead ...'

'Let's hear about Percival Fortescue.'

'Percival is a sly③ man. He's terrified of his father and has always let himself be bullied④.'

'And his wife?'

'Jennifer is quiet and seems very stupid. But she was a hospital nurse before her marriage — she nursed Percival when he had pneumonia⑤ and then he married her. Rex Fortescue disliked

---

① late *adj.* 过世的 ② bully *n.* 横行霸道者 ③ sly *adj.* 狡猾的
④ bully *v.* 欺负 ⑤ pneumonia *n.* 肺炎

poor Jennifer. She dislikes — disliked him a lot, I think. Her main interests are shopping and the cinema; her main complaint is that her husband, Percival, doesn't give her enough money.'

'What about the daughter?'

'Elaine? She's one of those schoolgirls who never grow up. There was some sort of romance with a young schoolmaster, Gerald Wright, but Mr Fortescue discovered the young man had communist① ideas and made them end the relationship.'

'She hadn't got the courage to stand up to② him?'

'*She* had. It was the young man who went away. I don't think he liked the idea that if she had married him, her father would have stopped giving her money to live on. Elaine is not particularly attractive.'

'And the other son?'

'I've never seen Mr Lance. He's attractive, everyone says, but a bad boy. He forged③ a cheque④ in the past. He lives in East Africa. Mr Fortescue couldn't throw him out of the business completely because he'd already made him a junior partner, but he hadn't kept in touch with him for years. All the same, I wouldn't be surprised if old Fortescue had been planning to get him back here. About a month ago, he discovered something that his eldest son, Percival, had been doing behind his back⑤— I don't know what it was — and he was furious.'

'Now, what about the servants? You've described the Crumps. Who else is there?'

'Gladys Martin is the parlourmaid⑥. She cleans the downstairs rooms, lays the table, clears away and helps Crump wait

---

① communist *adj*. 拥护共产主义的 ② stand up to 奋起反抗 ③ forge *v*. 伪造 ④ cheque *n*. 支票 ⑤ behind someone's back 背着某人 ⑥ parlourmaid *n*. 用餐女侍

at table. Quite a respectable sort of girl, but very stupid. Ellen Curtis is elderly and bad-tempered, but an excellent housemaid①.'

'And those are the only people living here?'

'There's old Miss Ramsbottom, Mr Fortescue's first wife's sister, who is well over seventy. She has a room on the second floor and never comes downstairs. She never liked her brother-in-law, but she came here while her sister was alive and stayed on when she died. Mr Fortescue isn't very interested in her. She's quite a character, though, is Miss Ramsbottom — or Aunt Effie as everyone calls her.'

'So we come to you, Miss Dove.'

'I'm an orphan②. I took a secretarial course and then a job as a shorthand typist. I decided I was in the wrong business, and started on my present career. I have been with three different employers. After about eighteen months I get tired of a place and move on. I have been at Yewtree Lodge for just over a year. I will type out the names and addresses of my previous employers and give them, with a copy of my references③, to Sergeant Hay.'

Neele was silent for a moment, enjoying a mental image of Miss Dove collecting yew berries in a little basket. With a sigh he returned to the present. 'Now, I would like to see Gladys Martin and then Ellen Curtis.' He added as he stood up, 'By the way, Miss Dove, can you give me any idea why Mr Fortescue would be carrying loose grain — rye, in fact — in his pocket?'

'Grain?' She stared at him.

'Yes — grain. Does that mean anything to you, Miss Dove?'

---

① housemaid *n*. 女佣 ② orphan *n*. 孤儿 ③ reference *n*. 推荐信

'Nothing at all.'

'Who looked after his clothes?'

'Crump.'

'I see. Did Mr Fortescue and Mrs Fortescue share the same bedroom?'

'Yes. He had a dressing room and bathroom, of course, and so did she ...' Mary looked down at her wristwatch. 'I really think that she ought to be back very soon now.'

The Inspector said in a pleasant voice, 'It seems to me very strange that even though there are three golf courses in the neighbourhood, it has not been possible to find Mrs Fortescue on one of them. Who was she playing with?'

'I think it is possible that it might be Mr Vivian Dubois.'

'I see.'

'I'll send Gladys in to you. She'll probably be scared to death.'

Mary Dove went out. Inspector Neele looked at the closed door. What she had told him was very useful. If Rex Fortescue had been deliberately poisoned, and it seemed almost certain that he had, then there appeared to be plenty of motives[①] at Yewtree Lodge.

---

① motive n. 动机

Chapter 5

The girl who entered the room looked a bit dirty in spite of being tall and smartly dressed in a dark red uniform. She said at once, anxiously, 'I didn't do anything. I didn't really. I don't know anything about it.'

'That's all right, Gladys,' said Neele in a comforting voice. 'Sit down here. I just want to know about breakfast this morning.'

He learnt little from her that he did not know already. Neele questioned her about herself and discovered that she had been in a private house first and after that had worked in various cafés. She had come to Yewtree Lodge in September. She had been there two months.

'Tell me about Mr Fortescue's clothes — his suits. Who took care of them?'

Gladys looked slightly annoyed. 'Mr Crump's supposed to. But half the time he makes me do it.'

'Have you ever found grain in the pocket of one of his suits? Rye, to be exact. There was some in the pocket of your master's① jacket. Do you know how it got there?'

'I couldn't say. I never saw any.'

He could get no more information from her. She certainly seemed uneasy② — but that was probably a natural fear of the police.

Inspector Neele went down to the kitchen where a very fat

---

① master n. 主人,雇主 ② uneasy adj. 不安的

woman stepped towards him in a threatening① way. 'Police!' she said. 'Any food that I've sent into the dining room has been just what it should be. How dare you② come here and say that I poisoned the master! No bad food has ever been served in this house.'

It was some time before Neele could reassure Mrs Crump that no one was accusing③ her of poisoning Rex Fortescue, then their conversation was ended by the ringing of the telephone.

Neele went out into the hall to find Mary Dove taking the call. She was writing down a message on a notepad. Turning her head she said, 'It's a telegram. The post office can't send anyone so they called instead ...'

She handed the notepad to the Inspector. The telegram had come from Paris and the message, addressed to Rex Fortescue, said:

I'm sorry but your letter to me was delayed. We will be with you tomorrow about teatime. I will expect roast beef for dinner. Lance.

'So the Bad Boy son *had* been asked to come home,' Inspector Neele said.

---

① threatening *adj.* 威胁的　② How dare you! 你怎么敢!　③ accuse *v.* 指控

Chapter 6

Inspector Neele was still holding the message when he heard a car drive up. Mary Dove said, 'That will be Mrs Fortescue now.'

As Inspector Neele moved forwards to the front door, he saw Mary Dove disappear.

The car was a Rolls Bentley① sports model. Two people came towards the house as Neele opened the front door. Surprised, Adele Fortescue stared at Inspector Neele, who realized at once that Adele Fortescue spoke and moved and breathed sex appeal. He then looked at the man behind her, who was carrying her golf clubs. He knew the type very well. They made their living② from the young wives of rich elderly men.

'Mrs Fortescue? I am Inspector Neele. I'm afraid I have bad news for you. Your husband became seriously ill this morning. We've been trying to contact you since half-past eleven. He was taken to St Jude's and I'm afraid you must prepare yourself for a shock.'

'You don't mean — he's — *dead*.' She fell forward a little and held onto his arm and the Inspector took her into the hall. Crump was there. 'She'll be needing brandy,' he said.

The deep voice of Mr Dubois said, 'That's right, Crump. Get the brandy.' To the Inspector he said, 'In here.' He opened the sitting room door and Adele Fortescue sat down on a chair, her eyes covered with her hand. She accepted the glass

---

① Rolls Bentley *n*. 劳斯莱斯-宾利(参见119页**文化注释**)　② make a living 谋生

that the Inspector offered a minute later and drank a tiny amount, then pushed it away. 'I don't want it. Tell me, what was it? A stroke①, I suppose? Poor Rex.'

'It wasn't a stroke. I'm afraid we need to find out as soon as possible exactly what Mr Fortescue had to eat or drink before he left for the office this morning.'

'Do you mean he might have been *poisoned*? I can't believe it. Oh — you mean *food* poisoning.'

His face showing nothing, Inspector Neele said, 'Madam? What did you think I meant?'

She ignored that question as Dubois said, looking at his watch, 'I must go, Adele. I'm very, very sorry. You'll be all right, won't you?'

'Oh, Vivian, don't. Don't go!' Adele Fortescue said.

'I'm really sorry but I've got an important meeting. I'm staying at the *Golf Hotel*, by the way, Inspector. If you — er — want me for anything.'

Inspector Neele nodded. Mr Dubois was clearly running away from trouble! Adele Fortescue said, 'I expect it's the awful bacon we get. It's quite uneatable sometimes.'

'We shall find out, Mrs Fortescue. You've got a lot of yew trees round the house. Is it possible that some of the berries or leaves got mixed up in any food or drink?'

Adele put her hands to her head. 'I don't want to talk about it! I can't stand any more. Mr Percival Fortescue will arrange everything. I can't ... I can't ... it isn't fair to ask me.'

'There's just one thing, Mrs Fortescue. There was a small amount of grain in your husband's pocket. Could you give me some explanation of that?'

---

① stroke *n*. 中风

She shook her head, puzzled.

'Would anyone have put it in there as a joke?'

'I don't see why it would be a joke.' She pulled out a handkerchief. 'It's so awful,' she said. 'Poor Rex. Poor dear Rex.' She began to cry as Inspector Neele watched her.

'It's been very sudden, I know,' he said. 'I'll send someone in to you.' He went towards the door and paused for a moment before looking back.

Adele Fortescue still held the handkerchief to her eyes. The ends of it hung down but did not quite hide her mouth. On her lips was a very small smile.

Chapter 7

'I've got what I could, Sir,' Sergeant Hay reported. 'The marmalade, a piece of the ham and samples① of tea, coffee and sugar. What they actually drank has been thrown away, of course, but there was a lot of coffee left over and the staff had it in the servants' hall.'

'So if the poison was in the coffee Fortescue drank, it must have been put into the actual cup by someone at the table,' said Neele.

The telephone rang and Neele nodded to Sergeant Hay, who went to answer it. It was Scotland Yard②. They had finally contacted Percival Fortescue, who was returning to London immediately. As the Inspector replaced the telephone receiver, a woman arrived at the front door, her arms full of parcels. Crump took them from her.

'Thanks, Crump. I'll have tea now. Is Mrs Fortescue or Miss Elaine in?'

The butler hesitated③. 'We've had bad news, ma'am,' he said. 'About the master.'

Neele came forward as she said, 'What's happened? An accident?' Mrs Jennifer Fortescue was a slightly overweight woman of about thirty. Her questions came with obvious interest.

'I'm sorry to tell you that Mr Rex Fortescue was taken to St Jude's Hospital. He was seriously ill and has since died,' Neele

---

① sample *n*. 样本 ② Scotland Yard *n*. 苏格兰场(伦敦警察厅总部)(参见 115 页**文化注释**) ③ hesitate *v*. 犹豫

said quietly.

'Died?' The news was clearly more exciting than sad. 'Dear me — are you from the office? You're not a doctor, are you?'

'I'm a police officer. Mr Fortescue's death was very sudden and ...'

She interrupted him. 'Do you mean he was *murdered*?' It was the first time that word had been spoken.

'Now why should you think that, Madam?'

'Well, you said sudden. And you're police. Have you seen *her* about it? What did *she* say?'

'Who are you talking about?'

'Adele, of course. He was completely under that awful woman's spell① — and now look what's happened ... What was it? Arsenic②?'

'The cause of death has not been decided yet. There will be an autopsy and an inquest.'

'But you know already, don't you? Or you wouldn't have come down here.' There was a sudden look of understanding in her rather silly face. 'You've been asking about what he ate and drank, I suppose?'

Neele said, 'It seems possible that Mr Fortescue's illness was caused by something he ate at breakfast.'

'Breakfast? I don't see how she could have done it, then ... unless she put something into the coffee — when Elaine and I weren't looking ...'

A quiet voice spoke softly, 'Your tea is in the library, Mrs Jennifer.'

Jennifer Fortescue jumped. 'Oh thank you, Miss Dove. What about you, Mr — Inspector ...'

---

① be under someone's spell 着了某人的魔　② arsenic *n*. 砒霜

'Thank you, no tea just now.'

Jennifer went slowly away as Mary Dove said quietly, 'I don't think she's ever heard of the word slander①. Is there anything I can do for you, Inspector Neele?'

'Where can I find the housemaid, Ellen?'

* * *

Ellen was as bad-tempered as Mary Dove had said she was, but she was also unafraid. 'It's a shocking business②, Sir. And I never thought I'd find myself in a house where such an awful thing has happened. But I can't say that it surprises me. Of course, I don't approve of what's been going on here. All this pretending to play golf — or tennis — and the library door was open one day and there they were, kissing.'

Neele really felt it unnecessary to say, 'Whom do you mean?' but he said it anyway.

'I mean Mrs Adele — and that man Dubois. You've been asking questions, Sir, about what the master ate and drank and who gave it to him. That Dubois found some kind of poison somewhere and *she* gave it to the master, I've no doubt.'

'Have you ever seen any yew berries in the house?'

'Yew? Nasty poisonous stuff. Don't you even *touch* yew berries, my mother said to me when I was a child. Was *that* what was used, Sir? Well, I've never seen her with yew berries.' Ellen sounded disappointed.

Neele questioned her about the grain found in Fortescue's pocket.

'No, Sir. I know nothing about that.'

---

① slander *n.* 诽谤   ② business *n.* 事情

Finally he asked if he could see Miss Ramsbottom, and Ellen took him upstairs. She knocked on a door, then opened it and said, 'There's a policeman here, an Inspector, who would like to speak to you, Miss.'

The room he entered was full of furniture and an old lady was sitting at a table in front of a gas fire, laying out cards in a game of patience①. Without looking up, she said impatiently, 'Well, come in, come in. What is it?'

'I'm sorry to tell you, Miss Ramsbottom, that your brother-in-law, Mr Fortescue, became ill and died this morning. I hope it's not a shock to you?'

Miss Ramsbottom looked at him sharply and said, 'Not at all. Rex Fortescue was always a sinful② man and I never liked him.'

'It seems possible that he may have been poisoned ...'

'Well, I didn't poison him, if that's what you want to know.'

'Have you any idea who might have done so?'

'Two of my dead sister's children are living in this house,' said the old lady. 'I refuse to believe that anybody with Ramsbottom blood in them could be guilty of murder. Because it *is* murder, isn't it? Plenty of people have wanted to murder Rex. He is — *was* — a very crooked③ man.'

'And is there anyone in particular you believe might have wanted to murder Mr Fortescue?'

Miss Ramsbottom collected her cards and rose to her feet. 'I think you'd better go now,' she said. 'If you want my opinion, it was probably one of the servants. Good evening.'

---

① patience *n*. 单人纸牌游戏 ② sinful *adj*. 有罪的 ③ crooked *adj*. 不诚实的

Inspector Neele found himself walking out without argument. He came down the stairs and came face to face with a tall, dark girl wearing a damp① raincoat.

'I've just come back,' she said. 'And they told me — that Father's dead.'

'I'm afraid that's true.'

Slowly two tears ran down her cheeks. 'It's awful,' Elaine Fortescue said. 'Do you know, I didn't think that I even liked him ... I thought I hated him ... But that can't be so, or I wouldn't be upset. And I am upset. The awful thing is that it makes everything alright. I mean, Gerald — my boyfriend — and I can get married now. But I hate it happening this way. I don't want Father to be dead ... Oh Daddy — Daddy ...'

For the first time since he had come to Yewtree Lodge, Inspector Neele was surprised by what seemed to be real grief② for the dead man.

---

① damp *adj.* 潮湿的 ② grief *n.* 悲伤

Chapter 8

Back at Scotland Yard, the Assistant Commissioner① had been listening to Neele giving his report. 'It sounds to me as if the wife murdered him,' said the Assistant Commissioner. 'What do you think, Neele, eh?'

Inspector Neele said that it looked like the wife to him, too.

'What about the other people in the house who had the opportunity?' asked the Assistant Commissioner.

'The daughter, Elaine, was involved with a young man, Gerald Wright, but her father didn't want her to marry him. And he definitely wasn't going to marry *her* unless she had money. That gives *her* a motive. As to the daughter-in-law, Jennifer, I don't know enough about her yet. But any one of the three of them *could* have poisoned him. The parlourmaid, the butler and the cook all handled the breakfast or brought it in, but I don't see how any of them could have been sure that Fortescue would get the taxine and nobody else. The butler and the parlourmaid both seem nervous, but there's nothing unusual about that with servants. The cook's angry and the housemaid was pleased. In fact, all quite natural and normal.'

'Is there anybody else who might be suspicious② in some way?'

'No, I don't think so, Sir.' Inspector Neele's mind went to Mary Dove, but aloud he said, 'Now that analysis has shown that it's definitely taxine, it should be possible to find some

---

① Assistant Commissioner *n*. 助理警察总监(参见 115 页**文化注释**)
② suspicious *adj*. 可疑的

evidence① as to how it was prepared.'

'Well, go ahead, Neele. By the way, Mr Percival Fortescue is waiting to see you. We've found the other son, Lance, too. He's in Paris, leaving today. You'll arrange for someone to meet him at the airport, won't you?'

'Yes, Sir.'

* * *

Mr Percival Fortescue was a neat, fair man of about thirty, with pale hair and eyelashes. 'This has been a terrible shock to me, Inspector Neele, as you can well imagine. I can only say that my father was perfectly well when I left. This food poisoning must have been very sudden?'

'It was very sudden, yes. But it wasn't food poisoning. Your father was poisoned by taxine.'

'Taxine? I've never heard of it.'

'Very few people have. It is a most unpleasant poison.'

'That's terrible!'

'Yes indeed, Mr Fortescue.'

'May I ask, do you have any ideas, any suspicions of who could ... Really, I ...' He broke off.

'It's rather soon for that, Mr Fortescue. It would be helpful if you could give us some idea of your father's will②.'

'My father made a new will when he got married two years ago,' said Percival. 'He left £100,000 to his wife and £50,000 to my sister, Elaine. I inherit③ everything else. I am already, of course, a partner in the firm.'

---

① evidence n. 证据 ② will n. 遗嘱(参见 122 页**文化注释**) ③ inherit v. 继承

'There was no bequest① to your brother, Lance?'

'No, my father had refused to have any contact with my brother for a long time.'

'So,' said Inspector Neele, 'the three people who inherit your father's fortune② are Mrs Adele Fortescue, Miss Elaine Fortescue and yourself?'

'I don't think there will be much of a fortune.' Percival sighed. 'There are death duties③, and lately my father had been behaving recklessly④ in some of his financial dealings.'

'You say your father and brother were not in touch with one another? Then perhaps you can tell me what *this* means?' Neele gave him the telephone message Mary Dove had written down.

Percival was surprised and annoyed. 'I can't understand it, I really can't. I can hardly believe it.'

'Your father said nothing to you about it?'

'He certainly did *not*. How outrageous⑤ of him. To go behind my back and send for Lance.'

'You've no idea, I suppose, *why* he did such a thing?'

'Of course I haven't. It's exactly like all his behaviour lately — crazy! It's got to be stopped. I ...' Percival came to a stop. The colour went from his already pale face. 'I had forgotten ... for a moment I had forgotten that my father was dead ...'

---

① bequest *n*. 遗产　② fortune *n*. 大笔钱财　③ death duties *n*. 遗产税
④ recklessly *adv*. 鲁莽地　⑤ outrageous *adj*. 令人吃惊的;不可接受的

Chapter 9

'It's quite amazing,' said Lance Fortescue. He stared at Detective Inspector Neele, who had met him and his wife at the airport and had taken them into a small office. Neele said, 'You've no idea then at all, who might have poisoned your father?'

'No. I expect the old man made a lot of enemies in business. But poisoning? Anyway, I've been abroad for years and know very little of what was going on at home.'

'Would you like to tell me why you came home at this time?'

'Certainly, Inspector. I heard from my father six months ago, soon after my marriage. He suggested that I came home and enter the firm. I came over to England three months ago and went down to see him at Yewtree Lodge. He made me a very good offer and I flew back to East Africa to discuss it with my wife, Pat. And I decided to accept the offer. I had to finish up my business there, and I told him I would send him a telegram with the date of my arrival in England.'

Inspector Neele coughed. 'This seems to have caused your brother some surprise.'

Lance's attractive face lit up with laughter. 'I believe Percival knew nothing about it,' he said. 'He was on holiday in Norway when I came over and I suspect① that my father made his offer to me because he had had a huge fight with poor Percival. It would be just the old man's idea of a good joke to bring me

---

① suspect v. 怀疑

home. However, as usual, Percy wins. I've arrived too late.'

'Yes,' said Inspector Neele thoughtfully. 'On your visit last August, did you meet any other members of the family?'

'My stepmother① was there at tea.' He grinned②. 'The old boy certainly knew how to choose a woman.'

'Were you upset about your father's remarriage?'

'I certainly wasn't. What I'm really surprised at, is that the old man didn't marry again before. Is that how it is, Inspector? Do you suspect my stepmother of poisoning my father?'

Inspector Neele's face became blank. 'It's early days to have any definite ideas about anything, Mr Fortescue,' he said pleasantly. 'Now, may I ask you what your plans are?'

'Where is the family? All down at Yewtree Lodge?'

'Yes.'

'I should go down there straight away.' He turned to his wife. 'And you should go and stay at the *Barnes's Hotel*, Pat. I'm not sure of my welcome — and I don't want to take you to a house where there's a poisoner around.'

---

① stepmother *n*. 继母　② grin *v*. 露齿笑

Chapter 10

Vivian Dubois tore up Adele Fortescue's letter angrily. Adele had telephoned him three times, and now she had written. On the whole, writing was far worse. He went to the telephone. 'Can I speak to Mrs Adele Fortescue, please?' A minute or two later he heard her voice.

'Vivian, at last! Oh, darling, the police have finally gone!'

'Yes, yes, but look here, Adele, we've got to be careful. *Don't telephone me and don't write.* Just for now, you understand? *We must be careful*. And Adele, my letters to you. You did burn them, didn't you?'

There was a moment's hesitation before Adele Fortescue said, 'Of course.'

'That's all right then. You'll hear from me soon.' He didn't like that hesitation. His letters were innocent① enough, he thought, but he could not be sure. Even if Adele had not already burnt his letters, would she have the sense to burn them now? Where did she keep them? Probably in that sitting room of hers upstairs in that fake② antique desk. She had said there was a secret drawer in it. Secret drawer! That wouldn't fool the police for long. But there were no police at the house now. They were probably busy looking for how Rex Fortescue was poisoned. They would not have done a room-by-room search of the house. It was possible that if he acted at once ...

---

① innocent *adj.* 无辜的   ② fake *adj.* 假的

*　*　*

Mary Dove paused at the window on the stairs, and in the late afternoon light outside noticed a man disappearing behind some bushes①. Was it Lance Fortescue, walking round the garden before coming in to face a possibly unfriendly family? In the hall she saw Gladys, who jumped in surprise when she saw her.

'Was that the telephone I heard just now?' Mary asked.

'Oh, that was a wrong number.' Gladys sounded breathless. 'And before that, it was Mr Dubois. He wanted to speak to the mistress.'

Mary said, 'Haven't you taken the tea in yet? It's twenty minutes to five. Bring it in now, will you?' Mary Dove went into the library and Gladys went to the kitchen, where Mrs Crump was making a pie. 'The library bell's been ringing and ringing. It's time you took in the tea, my girl.'

'All right, all right, Mrs Crump.'

Gladys went into the pantry②. She wasn't going to make sandwiches. They had cakes and biscuits and scones③ and honey. She had other things to think about. She made the tea in the silver pot, then carried the tea things on the big silver tray through to the library. She went back for the other tray with the food on it and had carried it as far as the hall, when the sudden ringing of the clock in the hall at five o'clock made her jump.

In the library, Adele Fortescue said sharply to Mary Dove, 'Where *is* everybody?'

---

① bush *n*. 灌木　② pantry *n*. 餐具室　③ scone *n*. 烤饼,司康饼

'I really don't know, Mrs Fortescue. Miss Elaine came in some time ago and I think Mrs Jennifer's writing letters in her room. I'll tell her that tea is ready.'

Going towards the door, she stood aside as Elaine Fortescue came into the room, then stopped for a moment in the hall. A large tray with cakes and scones on it was on one of the hall tables and she thought she heard Jennifer Fortescue walking upstairs. Nobody, however, came down the stairs and Mary went up and along the corridor. She knocked on a door and Mrs Jennifer's voice said, 'Come in.' Mary opened the door. 'Tea is just about to be served, Mrs Jennifer.' She was rather surprised to see Jennifer Fortescue taking off a warm coat. 'I didn't know you'd been out,' said Mary.

Jennifer sounded slightly out of breath. 'Oh, I was just in the garden, getting a little fresh air. But really, it was too cold.' Jennifer Fortescue followed Mary out of the room.

Downstairs in the hall, to Mary's surprise, the tray of food was still on the table. She was about to go and call Gladys when Adele Fortescue appeared in the door of the library, saying, 'Aren't we ever going to have anything to eat for tea?'

Quickly, Mary picked up the tray and took it in. She was carrying the empty tray out again when the front door bell rang. Mary went to the door. If this was Lance Fortescue at last, she was rather curious① to see him.

'How unlike the rest of the Fortescues,' Mary thought, as she looked up into the dark, handsome face. She said quietly, 'Mr Lance Fortescue?'

'Himself.'

Mary looked past him. 'Your luggage?'

---

① curious *adj.* 好奇的

'I've paid the taxi. This is all I've got.' He picked up a medium-sized bag.

'Oh, I thought you walked up. And your wife?'

'My wife won't be coming. At least, not just yet.'

'I see. Come this way, Mr Fortescue. Everyone is having tea.'

She took him to the library door and left him there. She thought to herself that Lance Fortescue was a very attractive man. A second thought followed the first, probably a great many other women thought so, too.

* * *

'Lance!' Elaine threw her arms round his neck with delight. He took them away gently and looked around the room.

'This is Jennifer?'

Jennifer Fortescue looked at him with curiosity. 'I'm afraid Percival's been delayed in town,' she said. 'He has to organize *everything*. You really have no idea what we're all feeling.'

'It must be terrible for you,' said Lance seriously, then he turned to the woman on the sofa, who was sitting with a piece of scone and honey in her hand.

'Of course,' cried Jennifer, 'you don't know Adele, do you?'

Lance said quietly, 'Oh yes, I do,' as he took Adele Fortescue's hand in his. As he looked down at her, her eyelids fluttered. She said in her lovely soft voice, 'Sit down here on the sofa beside me, Lance. I'm so glad you've come, we badly need another man in the house.'

Lance said, 'You must let me do everything I can to help.'

'The police here. They think ... they think ...' she broke off and cried out passionately①, 'Oh, it's awful! He was poisoned, and I really do believe they think it was one of *us*.'

Lance gave her a sudden quick smile. 'It's no good worrying,' he said, and changing the subject, exclaimed, 'Oh what a wonderful chocolate cake. I must have some.' Cutting himself a slice, he asked, 'Is Aunt Effie alive still?'

'Oh, yes, Lance. She won't come down and have meals with us, but she's quite well. Only she's getting very strange,' said Elaine.

'She always *was* strange,' said Lance. 'I must go up and see her after tea. And who's the young lady with the soft voice and sweet face who let me in? What goes on behind it, I wouldn't like to say.'

'That,' said Jennifer, 'is Mary Dove. She looks after everything for us.'

'Does she, now?'

Adele said, 'She's really very useful.'

'But what is so nice,' said Jennifer, 'is that she knows her place.'

'Clever Mary Dove,' said Lance, and took another piece of chocolate cake.

---

① passionately *adv.* 激动地

Chapter 11

'So *you've* turned up① again!' said Miss Ramsbottom.

Lance grinned at her. 'Just as you say, Aunt Effie.'

Miss Ramsbottom looked disapproving. 'Have you got your wife with you?'

'No. I left Pat in London.'

'That shows some sense. You never know what might happen *here*.'

'To Pat?'

'To anybody,' said Miss Ramsbottom.

Lance Fortescue looked at her thoughtfully. 'What's been going on here? What gives the police the idea that Father was killed in this house?'

'Adultery② is one thing and murder is another,' said Miss Ramsbottom. 'I would hate to think that she could kill someone.'

Lance looked alert. 'Adele?'

'I'm not saying anything else,' said Miss Ramsbottom, 'but I'll tell you one thing. I believe that girl knows something about it.'

'Which girl?'

'The one that never looks completely clean,' said Miss Ramsbottom. 'The one that should have brought up my tea this afternoon, but didn't. She's gone out without permission③, so Ellen told me. I wouldn't be surprised if she has gone to the police. Who let you in?'

---

① turn up 意外出现 ② adultery *n*. 通奸 ③ permission *n*. 许可

'Someone called Mary Dove. Is she the one who's gone to the police?'

'*Mary Dove* wouldn't go to the police,' said Miss Ramsbottom. 'No — I mean that silly little parlourmaid. She's been looking frightened all day. "What's the matter with you?" I said to her. "Have you got a guilty conscience①?" She said, "*I* never did anything — I wouldn't do a thing like that." Then she began to cry and said she didn't want to get anybody into trouble, she was sure it must all be a mistake. I said to her, "Now, my girl, you go to the police and tell them anything you know, because bad things happen when you hide the truth." Then she said she *couldn't* go to the police and said that anyway she didn't know anything at all.'

'You don't think that she was just making herself important?'

'No, I don't. She was scared. I think she saw something or heard something that's given her some idea about the whole thing. It may be important, or it may not.'

'The whole thing seems so strange. Like a detective story,' Lance said.

'Percival's wife used to be a hospital nurse,' said Miss Ramsbottom. 'Hospital nurses are used to handling drugs.'

Lance looked doubtful②.

'Family affection is one thing,' said Miss Ramsbottom, 'and I hope I've got as much of it as anyone. But I won't have wickedness③. Wickedness has to be destroyed.'

---

① guilty conscience *n*. 良心的谴责 ② doubtful *adj*. 不能肯定的
③ wickedness *n*. 恶劣

* * *

'Gladys went out without a word to me,' said Mrs Crump to Mary Dove. 'The master's dead, Mr Lance is coming home, and I said to Crump, "Day off or no day off, I know my duty. There's not going to be cold supper tonight as is usual on a Thursday, but a proper dinner." You know me, Miss, you know I like to do good work.'

Mary Dove nodded her head gently as Mrs Crump continued. 'And what did Crump say? "It's my day off and I'm going out," that's what he said. So out he went and I told Gladys she'd have to manage alone tonight. She just said, "All right, Mrs Crump," then *she* went out, without telling anyone.'

'We shall manage, Mrs Crump,' Mary's voice was comforting. 'I shall serve at table if Gladys doesn't come back in time.'

'*She* won't come back,' said Mrs Crump. 'She's got a young man, Miss, though you wouldn't think any man would be attracted to her with all those spots on her face! Albert his name is. They're going to get married next spring, so she tells me.' She sighed. 'What about tea things, Miss. Who's going to clear them away and wash them up?'

'I'll do that,' said Mary.

The lights had not been turned on in the library, though Adele Fortescue was still sitting on the sofa behind the tea tray.

'Shall I switch the lights on, Mrs Fortescue?' Mary asked.

Adele did not answer. Mary switched on the lights and it was only when she turned her head, that she saw the half-eaten scone spread with honey beside Adele, and her teacup still half full. Death had come to Adele Fortescue suddenly.

* * *

'Well?' demanded Inspector Neele.

The doctor said, 'Cyanide① — potassium cyanide probably — in the tea.'

Neele was angry. Poisoned! While he was in the house. Elaine had been the last to leave the library. According to her, Adele had been pouring herself a last cup of tea. And after that, it was twenty minutes until Mary Dove came into the room and discovered the body. Inspector Neele swore to himself and went out into the kitchen where Mrs Crump hardly moved as he came in. 'Where's that girl? Has she come back yet?'

'Gladys? No.'

'She made the tea, you say, and took it in.'

'Inspector Neele, I don't believe Gladys would do a thing like that — not Gladys. She's a bit silly, that's all — not wicked②.'

No, Neele did not think that Gladys was wicked. And the cyanide had not been in the teapot. 'But what made her go out suddenly — it wasn't her day off, you say.'

'No, Sir, tomorrow's her day off. But she had her best nylons③ on,' said Mrs Crump. 'So she was going to do something that wasn't connected with her work. Oh yes, she was up to something④. I'll give her a good telling-off⑤ when she comes back.'

When she comes back — Neele felt uneasy suddenly and

---

① cyanide *n*. 氰化物（参见 117 页**文化注释**）　② wicked *adj*. 恶劣的
③ nylon *n*. 尼龙袜　④ be up to something （准备）干……（尤指坏事）
⑤ telling-off *n*. 训斥

couldn't think why. He went upstairs to Adele Fortescue's sitting room. He had searched it carefully the day before and found the secret drawer in the desk. Now he made a small exclamation. On the centre of the carpet was a small piece of mud①. Neele went over and picked it up. It was still damp. He looked round — there were no footprints②— only this one bit of mud.

* * *

Inspector Neele looked round the bedroom that belonged to Gladys Martin. It was past eleven o'clock but there was still no sign of Gladys. Ellen, the housemaid, whose help he had wanted, had not been helpful. She didn't know what clothes Gladys owned, so she couldn't say what, if anything, was missing. He turned to the drawers where Gladys kept her treasures③. There were postcards and bits cut out of newspapers with hints on beauty, dressmaking and fashion advice.

Inspector Neele sorted them into groups. The postcards were mainly of views of places where he guessed Gladys had spent her holidays, but there were three from someone named 'Albert.' The first postcard said — in uneducated handwriting:

All the best. Missing you a lot. Yours ever, Albert.

The second one said:

Lots of nice-looking girls here, but not one that's as lovely as you. Be seeing you soon. Don't forget our date. And remember after that — we'll be living happy ever after.

The third just said:

---

① mud *n*. 泥 ② footprint *n*. 脚印 ③ treasures *n*. 珍爱之物

Don't forget. I trust you. Love, B.

Next, Neele looked through the pieces of newspaper and sorted them into three piles. There were the fashion and beauty hints, there were items about cinema stars, and she had also been interested in science. There were articles about secret weapons① and about truth drugs used by Russians to make people confess② to crimes. But there was nothing to give him a clue③ to her disappearance. She had kept no diary. Neele left the room, and as he went down the stairs he heard the noise of running feet. Then Sergeant Hay's worried face looked up at him from the bottom of the stairs.

'Sir,' he said urgently. 'Sir! We've found the parlour-maid! The housemaid, Ellen, remembered that she hadn't brought the clothes in from the washing line. So she went out with a torch and she almost fell over the girl's body — strangled④, she was, with a stocking⑤ round her throat — she's been dead for hours, I'd say. And, Sir, it's a wicked kind of joke — there was a *clothes peg*⑥ *on her nose* ...'

---

① weapon *n.* 武器　② confess *v.* 供认　③ clue *n.* 线索　④ strangle *v.* 勒死　⑤ stocking *n.* 女士长袜　⑥ clothes peg *n.* 晾衣夹

Chapter 12

Two days later Crump opened the door and saw a tall, elderly lady wearing an old-fashioned tweed① coat and skirt, a couple of scarves and a small hat with a bird's wing on it. An old but good quality suitcase was by her feet. Crump recognized a lady when he saw one and said, 'Yes, Madam?' in his most respectful voice.

'I have come,' Miss Marple said, 'to speak about the poor girl who was killed. Gladys Martin. Could I see the mistress of the house, please?'

'Oh, I see, Madam. Well in that case …' he looked towards the library door from which a tall young woman had just come out. 'This is Mrs Patricia Fortescue, Madam. I'm afraid Mr Percival's wife and Miss Elaine are out.'

Patricia came forward and Miss Marple was aware of a faint feeling of surprise. She had not expected to see someone like Patricia Fortescue in this luxuriously decorated house.

'It's about Gladys, Madam,' said Crump helpfully.

Pat said rather hesitantly, 'Will you come in here? We shall be completely alone.' She led the way into the library and Miss Marple followed her.

'My husband and I only came back from Africa a few days ago,' said Pat, 'and I only came to Yewtree Lodge yesterday, so I don't really know anything much about the household.'

Miss Marple looked at the girl and liked her. At the gymkhanas② held locally round her village, St Mary Mead, Miss

---

① tweed *adj*. 花呢的 ② gymkhana *n*. 赛马会

Marple had met many Pats and knew them well. She felt comfortable with this rather unhappy-looking girl.

'It's very simple, really,' said Miss Marple. 'I read in the paper, you see, about Gladys Martin having been killed. And of course I know all about her. I trained her, in fact, to be a parlourmaid. And since this terrible thing has happened to her, I felt — well, I felt that I ought to come and see if there was anything I could do about it.'

'Yes,' said Pat. 'Of course. I see.' And she did see at once just why Miss Marple needed to do something for a girl she had known so well. 'Nobody seems to know very much about her,' said Pat. 'I mean her relations and all that.'

'No,' said Miss Marple, 'she had no relations. She came to me from the orphanage①, *St Faith's*, and I taught her how to wait at table and look after the silverware. As soon as she got a little experience, she took a job in a café.'

'I never saw her,' said Pat. 'Was she a pretty girl?'

'Oh, no,' said Miss Marple. 'And she had bad skin. She was rather stupid, too. She was very interested in men, poor girl. But men didn't take much notice of her and other girls made use of her — got her to do things for them and were then unkind to her.'

'It sounds rather cruel②,' said Pat.

'Yes, my dear,' said Miss Marple, 'life is cruel, I'm afraid. Girls like Gladys enjoy going to the cinema and all that, but they're always dreaming of impossible things that can't possibly happen to them and they get disappointed. It was the clothes peg that made me so very angry. It was such a cruel thing to do! It's very wicked, you know, to show such disrespect. Particularly

---

① orphanage *n.* 孤儿院 ② cruel *adj.* 残忍的

if you've already killed.'

Pat said slowly, 'I believe I see what you mean. I think you should come and see Inspector Neele. He's a very human person.' She gave a sudden shiver①. 'The whole thing is such a horrible nightmare. Pointless. Mad. Without rhyme or reason② to it.'

'I wouldn't say that, you know,' said Miss Marple. 'No, I wouldn't say that.'

* * *

Inspector Neele was looking extremely tired and worried. Adele Fortescue, his main suspect③, was now the second victim in an unsolved murder case. But strangely, Inspector Neele had felt some satisfaction. The explanation that the wife and the lover had been responsible for Rex Fortescue's death had been too easy. He had always mistrusted④ it. And now that mistrust was confirmed⑤. He looked with interest at the gentle, serious face of the old lady who sat with him now at Yewtree Lodge.

'It's very good of you to come here, Miss Marple,' he said.

'It was my duty, Inspector Neele. The girl had lived in my house. I feel responsible for her. She was a very silly girl, you know.'

Inspector Neele looked at her with respect. She had gone, he felt, to the heart of the matter. 'When you say that she was silly …'

'She was the sort of girl who would give all her money to any man who told her she was beautiful and he needed it — if

---

① shiver *n*. 颤抖 ② rhyme or reason (某事的)规律或逻辑 ③ suspect *n*. 嫌疑犯 ④ mistrust *v*. 怀疑 ⑤ confirm *v*. 证实

she had any money. Of course, Gladys never did have any because she always spent it on most unsuitable clothes.'

'What about men?' asked the Inspector.

'She wanted a young man badly,' said Miss Marple. 'And I understand she got herself one in the end?'

Inspector Neele nodded. 'Albert Evans. She met him at some holiday camp. He was an engineer who worked in mines① abroad, so she told the cook.'

'That seems *most* unlikely,' said Miss Marple, 'but I am sure that is what he *told* her. You don't connect *him* with this business at all?'

Inspector Neele shook his head. 'No. He never seems to have visited her.'

'Well,' said Miss Marple, 'I'm pleased she had her little romance. Since her life has been cut short in this way ... I wonder — could I help you in my very small way? This is a wicked murderer, Inspector Neele, and the wicked should not go unpunished.'

'That's an unfashionable belief nowadays, Miss Marple,' Inspector Neele said. 'Not that I don't agree with you.'

'There is a hotel near the station,' said Miss Marple, 'and I believe there's a Miss Ramsbottom in this house who is interested in the work of foreign missions②. As I am. You know, help for poor people in Africa and India and so on. I believe we could have a good conversation about that — and other things ...'

Inspector Neele looked at Miss Marple with respect. 'Yes, I think that would be a great help. I can't say that I've had great success with the lady.'

---

① mine *n*. 矿井 ② foreign mission *n*. 外交使团

'It's really very kind of you, Inspector Neele,' said Miss Marple. 'I'm so happy you don't think I'm just being a curious old woman.'

Inspector Neele gave a sudden unexpected smile. Miss Marple seemed a very unlikely person to be helping him find a murderer. She continued speaking. 'Newspapers,' she said, 'so often make their reports more exciting than they really are.' She looked at Inspector Neele. 'Can you tell me the simple facts?'

'Mr Fortescue died in his office,' said Neele, 'as a result of taxine poisoning. Taxine comes from the berries and leaves of yew trees.'

'And Mrs Fortescue?'

'Adele Fortescue had tea with the family in the library. The last person to leave the room was Miss Elaine Fortescue, her stepdaughter. Twenty minutes later, Miss Dove, who is the housekeeper, went in to remove the tea tray. Adele was sitting on the sofa, dead. Beside her was a tea cup a quarter full and in it was potassium cyanide.'

'Such dangerous stuff,' said Miss Marple quietly. 'Gardeners keep it to destroy insect nests, but I'm always very, very careful.'

'You're quite right,' said Inspector Neele. 'There was a packet of it among the gardener's things.'

'Very convenient,' said Miss Marple. She added, 'Was Mrs Fortescue eating anything?'

'Oh, yes.'

'Cake, I suppose? Bread and butter? Jam? Honey?'

'There was honey and scones and chocolate cake.' He looked at her curiously. 'The potassium cyanide was in the tea, Miss Marple.'

'Oh, yes, yes. I understand that. I was just getting the whole picture. Rather significant①, don't you think?'

He looked at her, slightly puzzled. Her eyes were bright.

'And the third death, Inspector Neele?'

'Well, Gladys took in the tea tray, then she brought the next tray into the hall, but left it there. After that no one saw her. The cook, Mrs Crump, thought that the girl had gone out for the evening without permission. She thought that because the girl was wearing a good pair of nylon stockings and her best shoes. She was wrong. Gladys had obviously remembered suddenly that she had not taken in some clothes that were drying outside. She ran out to get them in and somebody put a stocking round her neck and — well, that was that. The girl was nervous, when we first questioned her, but I'm afraid we didn't think that meant anything.'

'Oh, but how could you?' cried Miss Marple. 'People so often do look guilty and uncomfortable when they are questioned by the police.'

'That's just it. But I think Gladys had seen someone doing something that she didn't understand — and I think she asked that person for an explanation.'

'And so Gladys was strangled and a clothes peg put on her nose,' Miss Marple said quietly.

'Yes, a nasty, unnecessary thing to do.'

Miss Marple shook her head. 'Hardly *unnecessary*. It does all make a pattern, doesn't it? First we have Rex Fortescue — killed in his office. And then we have Mrs Fortescue, sitting having tea. There were scones and *honey*. And then poor Gladys with the clothes peg on her nose. That very sweet Patricia Fortescue said that there seemed to be no rhyme or reason in it, but it's

---

① significant *adj.* 重要的

the rhyme that makes you think, isn't it?'

Inspector Neele said slowly, 'I don't think ...'

Miss Marple continued quickly, 'I expect you're about thirty-five or thirty-six, aren't you, Inspector Neele? I think that when you were a little boy, nursery rhymes① were out of fashion. But I was brought up② on them — and so, to me, it is really highly significant. What I wondered was ...' Miss Marple paused, then appearing to take her courage in her hands, continued, 'Of course I know I am very old and perhaps my idea is of no value at all, but what I mean to say is, have you thought about blackbirds③?'

---

① nursery rhyme *n*. 儿歌 ② bring up 抚养(儿童) ③ blackbird *n*. 乌鸫

Chapter 13

Inspector Neele's first thought was that the old lady had gone mad. 'Blackbirds?' he repeated.

Miss Marple nodded and said,

'*Sing a song of sixpence, a pocketful of rye,*
Four and twenty blackbirds baked in a pie.
When the pie was opened the birds began to sing.
Wasn't that a dainty① dish to set before the king?

The king was in his counting house, counting out his money,
The queen was in the parlour② eating bread and honey,
The maid was in the garden hanging out the clothes,
When there came a little dickey bird③ and nipped off④ her nose.'

'My goodness,' Inspector Neele said.

'I mean, it does fit,' said Miss Marple. '*Rex* Fortescue. Rex means *King*. In his *Counting House*, in other words at his place of work, dealing with money. And Mrs Fortescue, the *Queen in the parlour, eating bread and honey*. And so, of course, the murderer *had* to put that clothes peg on poor Gladys's nose.'

'You mean the whole thing is crazy?'

'Well, it is certainly very *strange*. But you really must make inquiries about blackbirds. Because there must *be* blackbirds!'

It was at this point that Sergeant Hay came into the room saying urgently, 'Sir.' He broke off at the sight of Miss Marple.

Inspector Neele said, 'Thank you, Miss Marple. I'll think

---

① dainty *adj.* 讲究的；秀丽的　② parlour *n.* 会客室　③ dickey bird *n.* (儿语)小鸟　④ nip off 咬掉

about what you've said. As you are interested in the girl, perhaps you would like to look at the things from her room. Sergeant Hay will show you them in a few minutes.'

Miss Marple nodded her head and went out.

'Blackbirds!' said Inspector Neele to himself. 'Yes, Hay, what is it?'

'Sir,' said Sergeant Hay. 'Look at this.' He showed him an object wrapped in a handkerchief. 'I found it in the bushes,' said Sergeant Hay. 'It could have been thrown there from one of the back windows.'

It was a nearly full pot of marmalade.

In his mind, the Inspector saw a new pot of marmalade; he saw hands carefully removing its cover; he saw a small amount of marmalade being removed, mixed with a preparation of taxine and replaced in the pot, the top smoothed over and the lid carefully replaced.

'And,' said Sergeant Hay, 'Mr Fortescue was the only one that had marmalade for breakfast. The others had jam or honey.'

Neele nodded. 'That made it very simple, didn't it?' In his mind he saw the breakfast table now. Rex Fortescue stretching out his hand for the marmalade pot, taking out a spoonful and puting it on his toast. And afterwards? The pot of marmalade being replaced by another with exactly the same amount taken from it. And then an open window. A hand and an arm throwing that pot out into the bushes. The only thing he couldn't see was whose hand and arm it was.

Inspector Neele said in a businesslike voice, 'Well, we'll have to get this analysed. How do they order marmalade and where is it kept?'

'Marmalade comes in six pots at a time. A new pot would be

taken into the pantry when the old one was nearly empty.'

'That means,' said Neele, 'that the taxine could have been put into the marmalade several days before it was actually put onto the breakfast table. And anyone who was *in* the house, or who could have got into the house, could have done it.'

Inspector Neele went to look for Mary Dove. She asked, 'Did you want to see me about something?'

Neele said pleasantly, 'It's becoming important to get exact times clear. Members of the family all seem a little unsure about times. You, Miss Dove, have been extremely accurate. Now, the last time you saw Gladys Martin was in the hall before tea, and that was at twenty minutes to five?'

'Yes.'

'Where were you coming from?'

'From upstairs — I had heard the telephone.'

'Gladys had answered the telephone?'

'Yes. It was a wrong number,' said Miss Dove.

'And that was the last time you saw her?'

'She brought the tea tray into the library about ten minutes later.'

'After that Miss Elaine Fortescue came in?'

'Yes, about three minutes later. Then I went up to tell Mrs Jennifer tea was ready.'

'Did you usually do that?' Neele asked.

'No — people came in to tea when they pleased — but Mrs Adele Fortescue asked where everybody was. I thought I heard Mrs Jennifer coming — but that was a mistake ...'

Neele interrupted. 'You mean you heard someone upstairs moving about?'

'Yes — but no one came down, so I went up. Mrs Jennifer was in her bedroom. She had been out for a walk.'

'The time was then ... ?' asked Neele.

'Oh — nearly five o'clock.'

'And Mr Lance Fortescue arrived — when?'

'A few minutes after I came downstairs — I thought he had arrived earlier — but ...'

Inspector Neele interrupted, 'Why did you think he had arrived earlier?'

'Because I thought I had seen him through the window. I caught a glimpse① of someone through the yew bushes — and I thought it would be him.'

'This was when you were coming down after telling Mrs Jennifer Fortescue tea was ready?'

Mary corrected him, 'No, when I came down the first time.'

Inspector Neele kept his inner excitement out of his voice as he said, 'It couldn't have been Lance Fortescue. His train arrived at Baydon Heath at 4.37. He had to wait for a taxi. It was actually nearly a quarter to five (five minutes *after* you had seen the man in the garden) when he left the station and it is a ten-minute drive. He paid the taxi at the gate here at about five minutes to five at the earliest.'

'I'm sure I did see someone.'

'He was going — which way?'

'Along behind the yew bushes towards the east side of the house.'

'There is a side door there. Is it kept locked?'

'Not until the house is locked up for the night.'

'Anyone could have come in by that side door without being seen by any of the household?'

---

① glimpse *n.* 一瞥

'Yes.' She added quickly, 'You mean — the person I heard later upstairs could have come in that way? Could have been hiding — upstairs? But who ... ?'

'That we have to find out. Thank you, Miss Dove.'

As she turned to go, Inspector Neele said in a casual voice, 'By the way, you can't tell me anything about *blackbirds*, can you?'

For the first time Mary Dove looked surprised. 'You mean that silly business last summer? It must, I think, have been some nasty joke. Four dead blackbirds were on Mr Fortescue's desk in his study here, and then more were found in a pie.'

'Any sort of reason behind it — any connection with blackbirds?'

Mary shook her head. 'I don't think so.'

'Was Mr Fortescue annoyed?'

'Of course.'

'But he was not upset in any way?'

'I really can't remember.'

'I see,' said Inspector Neele.

Mary Dove once more turned away, but this time, he thought, she went slowly, as if she would like to know more of what was in his mind. Well, Miss Marple had suggested that there would be blackbirds and, sure enough, there the blackbirds were! Inspector Neele was not going to let this blackbird business take his attention away from the logical investigation① of murder by a sane② murderer for a sane reason. But of course he would still consider the crazier possibilities of the case.

---

① investigation *n*. 调查 ② sane *adj*. 神智健全的

Chapter 14

What Mary Dove had said about hearing someone moving about upstairs explained the small piece of mud Neele had found on the floor of the sitting room. He thought of the pretty desk in that room with its obvious 'secret' drawer.

He had found three letters in that drawer, written by Vivian Dubois to Adele Fortescue. Neele had sent them up at once to the Yard because at that time it looked as if Rex Fortescue had been poisoned by his wife, with or without her lover's help. But there had been nothing in any of the letters to suggest that a crime was being planned. Inspector Neele believed that Dubois had asked Adele to destroy his letters and that she had told him she had done so.

Well, now they had two more deaths to investigate. That should mean that Adele Fortescue had not killed her husband. Unless Adele Fortescue had wanted to marry Vivian Dubois and Vivian Dubois had wanted, not Adele, but the hundred thousand pounds which would come to her on the death of her husband. He had believed, perhaps, that Rex Fortescue's death would be blamed① on natural causes.

What if Adele Fortescue and Vivian Dubois *had* been guilty? Adele might have rung up Dubois, talking loudly and he had realized that someone in Yewtree Lodge might have overheard her. What would Vivian Dubois have done next?

Inspector Neele decided to make inquiries at the *Golf Hotel* to find out if Dubois had been in or out of the hotel between the

---

① blame *v.* 怪罪

hours of quarter past four and six o'clock. Vivian Dubois was tall and dark like Lance Fortescue. He might have gone through the garden to the side door, gone upstairs and then what? Looked for the letters and found them missing? Or maybe waited until tea was over and then gone down to the library when Adele Fortescue was alone?

But all this was going too fast; he must see what Jennifer Fortescue had to say.

Chapter 15

Jennifer Fortescue was in her own sitting room upstairs, writing letters.

'I'm afraid,' Neele said comfortingly, 'we have to ask people questions again and again, and so much depends on the exact *timing* of events. You came down to tea late, I understand? In fact, Miss Dove came up to get you.'

'Yes, she did. I had no idea it was so late. I had been writing letters.'

'I see,' he said. 'I thought you had been out for a walk.'

'Did she say so? Yes — I believe you're right. I felt I needed some fresh air and I went out and — er — went for a walk. Only round the garden.'

'I see. You didn't meet anyone?'

'Meet anyone? I saw the gardener in the distance, that's all.' She was looking at him suspiciously.

'Then you came in, and you were just taking your coat off when Miss Dove came to tell you that tea was ready?'

'Yes. Yes, and so I came down. We had tea. Then Lance went up to see Aunt Effie and I came up to finish my letters. I left Elaine with Adele.'

Neele nodded. 'Yes. Miss Elaine seems to have been with Mrs Adele Fortescue for five or ten minutes after you left. Your husband hadn't come home yet?'

'Oh no. Percival didn't get home until about half-past six or seven.'

'I see,' said Inspector Neele. 'I asked your husband if Mrs Fortescue had made a will before she died. He said he thought not. I suppose *you* don't happen to have any idea?'

'Oh, yes,' she said, to his surprise. 'Adele made a will about a month ago. I saw her coming out of the solicitor's[①] office, *Ansell and Worrall's*, in the High Street. And I said to her, "Whatever have you been doing there?" And she laughed and said, "I've been making my will. Everyone ought to make a will." She hadn't wanted to go to the family solicitor in London, Mr Billingsley. "No," she said, "my will's my own business, Jennifer, and nobody's going to know about it." "Well," I said, "*I* won't tell anybody." And I didn't tell anyone, not even Percival.'

'Well, thank you very much, Mrs Fortescue, for being so helpful to me,' said Inspector Neele. 'There's one other thing, Mrs Fortescue. Do you know anything about blackbirds?'

Jennifer Fortescue looked shocked. 'Blackbirds, Inspector? What kind of blackbirds?'

'Just blackbirds. Alive or dead or even, shall we say, in a nursery rhyme?'

She said slowly, 'I suppose you mean the ones last summer in the pie. All very silly.'

'There were some left on the library table, too, weren't there?'

'It was all a very silly joke. Mr Fortescue, my father-in-law, was very much annoyed by it. He asked us if there were any strangers about the place.'

'Strangers? Did he seem afraid in any way?'

'Yes. Yes, he did.'

---

① solicitor *n*. 律师

* * *

Percival Fortescue was in London, but Inspector Neele found his brother Lance sitting with his wife Pat in the library.

'Do you know anything about blackbirds, Mr Fortescue?'

'Blackbirds?' Lance looked amused. 'Do you mean real birds?'

Inspector Neele said with a sudden, sweet smile, 'I'm not sure what I mean, Mr Fortescue. It's just that blackbirds have been mentioned.'

'Good Lord. Not the old Blackbird Mine, I suppose?'

'The Blackbird Mine? What was that?'

Lance frowned①. 'I just have an idea about some unpleasant business in my papa's past, on the west coast of Africa. Aunt Effie once mentioned it when she was having an argument with him, but I can't remember much about it.'

'I'll go and ask her about it,' said Inspector Neele, adding, 'She's rather a frightening old lady.'

Lance laughed. 'Yes. But she may be helpful to you, Inspector. I went up to see her, you know, soon after I got back here. And she was talking about Gladys, the maid who got killed. Not that we knew she was dead then, of course. But Aunt Effie was saying she was quite sure that Gladys knew something that she hadn't told the police.'

'That seems fairly certain,' said Inspector Neele. 'She'll never tell it now, poor girl.'

To his surprise, when he went up to see Miss Ramsbottom, he found Miss Marple with her, discussing foreign missions.

---

① frown v. 皱眉

'I'll go away, Inspector.' Miss Marple rose to her feet.

'No need, Madam,' said Inspector Neele.

'I've asked Miss Marple to come and stay,' said Miss Ramsbottom. 'There is no sense in her spending her money in that *Golf Hotel*. It's a wicked place. Drinking and card playing all the evening. She had better come and stay in a respectable household. There's a room next door to mine.'

'It's very kind of you,' said Miss Marple gratefully. 'I'll go and cancel my booking.' She left the room and Miss Ramsbottom said sharply to the Inspector, 'Well, and what do *you* want?'

'I wondered if you could tell me anything about the Blackbird Mine, Madam.'

Miss Ramsbottom gave a shout of laughter. 'Ha. You've got on to *that*, have you! Well, what do you want to know about it?'

'Anything you can tell me, Madam.'

'I can't tell you much. It's a long time ago now — oh, twenty to twenty-five years maybe, in East Africa. My brother-in-law went into business with a man called MacKenzie. They went out there to investigate the mine together and MacKenzie died of fever①. Rex came home and said there was no gold in the mine. That's all *I* know.'

'I think you know a little more than that, Madam,' said Neele.

'Well, the MacKenzies insisted that Rex had cheated② MacKenzie and he probably had, but they couldn't prove anything. Mrs MacKenzie came here and said Rex had murdered her husband. I think she was a bit mad — in fact, I believe she went

---

① fever *n.* 发烧 ② cheat *v.* 欺诈

into a hospital for the insane① not long after. She came here with a couple of young children who looked scared to death. She said she would bring up her children to get revenge②. Madness, all of it. Well, that's all I can tell you. And the Blackbird Mine wasn't the only bad thing that Rex did in his lifetime. You'll find a good many more if you look for them.'

'You don't know what happened to the MacKenzie family, Madam?'

'No idea,' said Miss Ramsbottom. 'And I don't think Rex would have actually murdered MacKenzie, but he might have left him to die. If he did, then he's been paid back. You should go away now, I can't tell you any more.'

'Thank you very much for what you *have* told me,' said Inspector Neele.

'Send that Marple woman back,' Miss Ramsbottom called after him. 'She knows how to organize things properly.'

Inspector Neele made a couple of telephone calls, the first to Adele Fortescue's lawyers, *Ansell and Worrall* and the second to the *Golf Hotel*, then he told Sergeant Hay, 'I have to visit a solicitor's office — after that, you can find me at the *Golf Hotel* if anything urgent happens.'

---

① insane *adj.* 精神失常的 ② revenge *n.* 复仇

Chapter 16

Mr Ansell was anxious to help the police in every way possible. Yes, he said, he had made a will for the late Mrs Adele Fortescue. He had not done any legal business before that for Mrs Fortescue or for any of the Fortescue family. 'Naturally,' said Mr Ansell, 'she didn't want to go to her husband's firm of lawyers.'

The facts were simple. Adele Fortescue had made a will leaving everything she possessed to Vivian Dubois.

'But I understood,' said Mr Ansell, 'that she didn't actually have much to leave.'

Inspector Neele nodded. At the time Adele Fortescue made her will that was true. But since then Rex Fortescue had died, and Adele Fortescue had inherited £100,000 and that now belonged to Vivian Edward Dubois.

* * *

At the *Golf Hotel*, Inspector Neele found Vivian Dubois nervously waiting for him.

'I do hope you realize, Inspector Neele, that it is very inconvenient for me to have to stay on. I really have important business.'

'I didn't know you were in business, Mr Dubois,' said Inspector Neele in a friendly way. 'Mrs Fortescue's death must have been a terrible shock to you. You were great friends, were you not?'

'Yes, the whole thing is terrible.'

'You actually telephoned her, I believe, on the afternoon of her death? About four o'clock. Do you remember what your conversation was about, Mr Dubois?'

'I think I asked her how she was feeling and if there was any further news about her husband's death — a more or less ordinary inquiry.'

'I see,' said Inspector Neele. 'And then you went out for a walk?'

'Er — not a walk, I went and played golf.'

'I think not, Mr Dubois. The doorman here saw you walking down the road towards Yewtree Lodge.'

Dubois's eyes met his, then moved away again nervously. 'I'm afraid I can't remember, Inspector.'

'Perhaps you actually went to visit Mrs Fortescue?'

Dubois said sharply, 'No. No. I never went near the house.'

'Where did you go, then?'

'Oh, I ... down the road as far as the pub①, The Three Pigeons, and then I turned around and came back by the golf course.'

The Inspector shook his head. 'You know, Mr Dubois,' he said pleasantly, 'I think we'll have to ask you for a statement② and perhaps you should have a solicitor present.'

The colour left Dubois' face. 'You're threatening me! I had nothing to do with it at all, I tell you! Nothing!'

'Come now, Mr Dubois, you were at Yewtree Lodge about half-past four on that day. Somebody saw you. Didn't you go in by the side door and up the stairs to Mrs Fortescue's sitting room? You were looking for something in the desk there?'

'*You've* got the letters, I suppose,' said Dubois. 'But they

---

① pub *n*. 酒吧 ② statement *n*. 证词

don't mean what you think they mean.'

'You're not denying①, are you, that you were a very *close* friend of Mrs Fortescue's?'

'No — but don't think that we — that she — ever thought of killing Rex Fortescue. I'm not *that* kind of man!'

'But perhaps she was that kind of woman?'

'Nonsense! Wasn't she killed, too? So didn't the same person who killed her husband kill her?'

'Possibly. But it's also possible that Mrs Fortescue murdered her husband, and that after his death she became a danger to someone else. Someone who had, perhaps, not helped her with what she had done but who had at least encouraged her and provided the *motive*. She might be a danger to that person.'

Dubois said nervously, 'You can't build up a case against me. You can't.'

'She left all her money to you.'

'I don't want the money!'

'Of course, it isn't very much,' said Inspector Neele.

'But I thought her husband ...' He stopped dead.

'Did you, Mr Dubois?' said Inspector Neele, and there was no friendliness now in his voice. 'That's very interesting. I wondered if you knew exactly what Rex Fortescue's will said.'

* * *

Inspector Neele's second interview at the hotel was with Mr Gerald Wright, a very superior young man, not unlike Vivian Dubois in appearance.

'What can I do for you, Inspector Neele?' he asked.

---

① deny *v*. 否认

'I thought you might be able to help us with a little information, Mr Wright, in connection with the recent events at Yewtree Lodge.'

'I know nothing. I was actually in the Isle of Man when Mr Rex Fortescue was killed.'

'You arrived here very shortly afterwards, Mr Wright. You had a telegram, I believe, from Miss Elaine Fortescue. And you are, I understand, to be married?'

'Quite right, Inspector Neele.'

'I understand that Mr Fortescue refused to give his permission and told you that if his daughter married against his wishes, he would not give her any money to live on. You then broke off the engagement.'

Gerald Wright smiled. 'Not exactly true, Inspector Neele. Actually, Rex Fortescue was a capitalist① and my political beliefs would not let me live off his money.'

'But you have no objection② to marrying a woman who has just inherited £50,000?'

Gerald Wright gave a satisfied smile. 'Not at all, Inspector Neele. The money will be used to help other people.'

'Mr Wright, Mrs Adele Fortescue died as a result of cyanide poisoning on the afternoon of November 5th. As you were in the neighbourhood of Yewtree Lodge on that afternoon, I thought you might have seen or heard something that might help our investigations.'

'And why do you believe that I was in the neighbourhood of Yewtree Lodge?'

'You left this hotel at a quarter-past four. After you left the hotel you walked down the road towards Yewtree Lodge. It

---

① capitalist *n*. 资本家　② objection *n*. 反对

seems natural to believe that you were going there.'

'I already had an arrangement to meet Elaine at the hotel at six. I went for a walk and returned to the hotel just before six o'clock. Elaine, quite naturally, did not keep her appointment.'

'Did anybody see you on this walk, Mr Wright?'

'No one I knew.'

'So I've only got your word that you were where you say you were?'

Gerald Wright continued to smile in a superior way, 'Very sad for us both, Inspector, but there it is.'

Inspector Neele said softly, 'Then if someone said they looked out of a window and saw you in the garden of Yewtree Lodge at about four thirty-five ...' He paused and left the sentence unfinished.

Gerald Wright shook his head. 'It was getting dark by then. I think it would be difficult for anyone to be sure.'

'Do you know Mr Vivian Dubois, who is also staying here?'

'Dubois? Is that the tall, dark man who wears very brightly coloured ties?'

'Yes. He also was out for a walk that afternoon. You did not notice him in the road by any chance?'

'No. No. I can't say I did.' Gerald Wright looked for the first time slightly worried.

Inspector Neele said thoughtfully, 'It wasn't really a very nice afternoon for walking, especially after dark. It's strange how full of energy everyone seems to have felt.'

Chapter 17

'So you're Lance's wife,' Miss Ramsbottom said. 'You're a tall girl and you look healthy. Where did you meet my nephew?'

'In Kenya, when I was staying with some friends,' Pat replied.

'You've been married before, I understand.'

'Yes. Twice. My first husband was a fighter pilot. He was killed in the war.'

'And your second husband shot himself. Was it your fault?'

'No,' said Pat. 'It wasn't my fault.'

'He was a horse-racing man, wasn't he?'

'Yes.'

'I've never been to a horse race in my life,' said Miss Ramsbottom. 'Gambling① and card playing — all evil! Ah, well, it's a wicked world nowadays. A lot of wickedness was going on in this house, but they got what they deserved. I'll tell you this. My sister Elvira was a fool, my brother-in-law Rex was a horrible man, Percival is nasty, and your Lance was always the bad boy of the family. Don't trust Percival. I've never liked him. Mind you, I don't *trust* Lance, but I can't help being fond of him. He's a reckless sort of boy — always has been. You've got to look after him and see he doesn't go too far. Tell him not to believe everything that Percival says. They're all liars in this house.'

---

① gambling *n*. 赌博

* * *

The triple tragedy① at Yewtree Lodge had shocked the Fortescues' lawyer, Mr Billingsley. He was only too anxious to help the police. 'It's a most extraordinary business. I'll tell you whatever I can.'

'First let me ask you how well you knew Mr Rex Fortescue, and how well you know the affairs of his firm.'

'I've known Rex Fortescue for sixteen years — although we are not the only firm of solicitors he employed.'

Inspector Neele nodded. *Billingsley, Horsethorpe & Walters* were respectable solicitors. For his less honest business, Rex Fortescue had employed less honest firms.

'Now what do you want to know?'

'I'm interested in the will of his widow. On Mr Fortescue's death she inherited the sum of one hundred thousand pounds, I understand?'

Billingsley nodded. 'A large amount of money. And one the firm would have found difficult to pay out.'

'The firm is not doing well?'

'Well, *Consolidated Investments Trust* was doing very well, buying and selling stocks and shares② wisely. But for the last year Rex Fortescue had been acting like a madman. Selling good stock here, buying very questionable projects there. Really, he seemed to have been a changed man.'

'But not, I understand, a depressed③ man,' said Inspector Neele.

---

① tragedy *n*. 悲剧 ② stocks and shares *n*. 股票与证券 ③ depressed *adj*. 消沉的

'No, no. The opposite. He had become very overexcited and convinced only *he* knew how to run the firm.'

Inspector Neele nodded. An idea was forming in his mind.

Mr Billingsley was continuing, 'But it's no good asking me about the wife's will. *I* didn't make any will for her.'

'I know that,' said Neele. 'I'm simply checking that she had a hundred thousand pounds from Rex Fortescue's will to leave.'

Mr Billingsley was shaking his head. 'No, no, my dear Sir. She did not inherit the hundred thousand pounds unless she lived for one month after his death.'

Inspector Neele was staring at him. 'Then what happens to that money?'

'It goes to Mr Percival Fortescue. And with the firm in a poor condition, I would say that he'll need it!'

Chapter 18

In the drawing room at Yewtree Lodge, the whole Fortescue family was together.

'I think we might discuss future plans,' said Percival. 'I suppose you'll be off again back to Kenya — or Canada — or climbing Mount Everest or something fairly exciting, Lance?'

'Now what makes you think that?' Lance smiled. 'I'm coming into the firm with you. I *have* got the share in it that Father gave me years ago and that gives me the right to be involved, doesn't it?'

Percival frowned. 'Things are in a very bad way, you know. We'll only just be able to pay Elaine her share, if she insists on having it. So are you serious, Lance?'

'Completely serious.'

'It won't work! You'll soon get bored,' Percival said.

'Why are you so angry, dear brother? Don't you look forward to having me sharing your problems?'

'You haven't the slightest idea of the mess everything's in,' replied Percival. 'For the last six months — no, a year, Father was not himself. He sold good stock and bought some very strange investments.'

'In fact,' said Lance, 'it's just as well for the family that he had taxine in his tea.'

'That's a very ugly way of putting it, but it's about the only thing that saved us from bankruptcy①. We shall have to be very careful for a while.'

---

① bankruptcy *n*. 破产

Lance shook his head. 'I don't agree with you. We must take a few risks, go for something big.'

Percival walked up and down angrily. 'It's no good, Lance. Our ways of doing business are totally different. The only sensible thing is to end the partnership.'

'You're going to buy me out — is that the idea?'

'Well, I didn't mean in cash,' said Percival. 'We could — er — divide everything up.'

'With you keeping the best bits and me getting the mad investments Father bought recently, I suppose?'

'They seem to be what you prefer,' said Percival.

Lance grinned. 'You're right in a way, old boy. But I've got Pat here to think of.'

Pat opened her mouth, then shut it again. Whatever game Lance was playing, it was best that she did not become involved.

'So what *are* you planning to give me?' said Lance, laughing. 'Diamond mines that have no diamonds, the oil fields where no oil has been found? Do you think I'm quite as big a fool as I look?'

Percival said, 'Of course, some of these things that Father bought have turned out to be worthless, but some of them *may* turn out to be very valuable.'

Lance grinned. 'Are you going to offer me the old Blackbird Mine as well? By the way, has the Inspector been asking you about this Blackbird Mine?'

Percival frowned. 'Yes, he did. I couldn't tell him much. You and I were children at the time. I just remember that Father went out there and came back saying the whole thing was no good.'

'What was it — a gold mine?'

'I believe so. Father came back certain that there was no gold there.'

'Who involved him in it? A man called MacKenzie, wasn't it? And MacKenzie died out there. I seem to remember ... Mrs MacKenzie, wasn't it? She came here and accused Father of murdering her husband.'

'Really?' said Percival. 'I can't remember anything like that.'

'I do, though,' said Lance. 'Where was Blackbird? West Africa wasn't it?'

'Yes, I think so.'

'I must find the paperwork on it sometime,' said Lance, 'when I'm at the office.'

'You can be quite sure,' said Percival, 'that if Father came back saying there was no gold, there was no gold.'

'You're probably right there,' said Lance. 'Poor Mrs MacKenzie. I wonder what happened to her and to those two kids she brought along. Funny — they must be grown up by now.'

Chapter 19

At the *Pinewood Private Sanatorium*①, Inspector Neele was facing a grey-haired lady. Helen MacKenzie was sixty-three, though she looked younger. She was holding a large book and was looking down at it as Inspector Neele talked to her.

'She's a voluntary② patient,' Dr Crosbie, the sanatorium's director, had told him. 'Most of the time she's as sane as you or me. It's one of her good days today, so you'll be able to have a completely normal conversation with her.'

Inspector Neele said now, 'It's very kind of you to see me, Madam. My name is Neele. I've come to see you about a Mr Rex Fortescue, who has recently died. I expect you know the name.'

Mrs MacKenzie said, 'I don't know what you're talking about.'

'I think, Mrs MacKenzie, you knew him many years ago.'

'Not really,' said Mrs MacKenzie. 'It was yesterday.'

'I see,' said Inspector Neele. 'I believe that you paid him a visit many years ago at Yewtree Lodge.'

'A house decorated with money, but no taste,' said Mrs MacKenzie.

'He had been connected with your husband, I believe, over a certain mine in Africa. The Blackbird Mine?'

'It was my husband's mine. He found it and wanted money to get the gold out. He went to Rex Fortescue.'

'And they went out together to Africa, and your husband

---

① sanatorium *n*. 疗养院 ② voluntary *adj*. 自愿的

died of fever.'

'I must read my book,' said Mrs MacKenzie.

'Do you think Mr Fortescue cheated your husband over the Blackbird Mine, Mrs MacKenzie?'

Without raising her eyes from the book, Mrs MacKenzie said, 'How stupid you are.'

'Yes, yes, perhaps ... But you see, finding out about a thing that was over a long time ago is rather difficult.'

'Who said it was over? Nobody knows where my husband died or how he died or where he was buried. All anyone knows is what Rex Fortescue *said*. And Rex Fortescue was a liar!'

'Somebody put dead blackbirds on Rex Fortescue's desk about a month or two before he died. Have you any idea who might have done that?'

'Ideas aren't any help to anyone. There has to be action. I brought them up to take action. Donald and Ruby. They were nine and seven and left without a father. I told them every day. I made them promise every night.'

Inspector Neele leant forward. 'What did you make them promise?'

'That they would kill him, of course.'

Inspector Neele spoke as though it was the most reasonable comment in the world. 'Did they?'

'Donald went to fight in France. They sent me a telegram saying that he had been killed in action[①]. Action, you see, the wrong kind of action.'

'I'm sorry to hear that, Madam. What about your daughter?'

'Do you know what I've done to Ruby? Look here at the Book.'

---

① killed in action 阵亡

He saw then that what she was holding in her lap was a very old family Bible in which the old-fashioned custom had been continued of entering each new birth. Mrs MacKenzie pointed to the last two names. *Donald MacKenzie* with the date of his birth, and *Ruby MacKenzie* with the date of hers. But a thick line was drawn through Ruby MacKenzie's name.

'You see?' said Mrs MacKenzie. 'I crossed her out of the Book. She doesn't exist anymore!'

'Why, Madam?'

Mrs MacKenzie looked at him slyly. 'She didn't do as I said.'

'Where is your daughter now, Madam?'

'There isn't such a person as Ruby MacKenzie any longer.' Mrs MacKenzie refused to say more and Neele had another short interview with Dr Crosbie.

'Do any of her relations come to see her?' he asked.

'I believe a daughter did come to see her before my time here, but her visit upset the patient so much that they advised her not to come again. Since then everything has been arranged through solicitors.'

Inspector Neele had already been to see those solicitors. They were unable, or said they were unable, to tell him anything. A trust fund① had been arranged for Mrs MacKenzie, which they managed.

'So there we are, Sir,' said Inspector Neele as he reported to the Assistant Commissioner. 'It's crazy, but it all fits together. It *must* mean something.'

The Assistant Commissioner nodded. 'The blackbirds in the pie and the Blackbird Mine, rye in the dead man's pocket,

---

① trust fund *n.* 信托基金

bread and honey with Adele Fortescue's tea, that girl strangled with a stocking and a clothes peg put on her nose. Yes, crazy as it all is, it certainly can't be ignored.'

'Half a minute, Sir,' said Inspector Neele.

'What is it?'

Neele was frowning. 'You know, what you've just said. It was wrong somewhere.' He shook his head. 'No. I can't see it.'

Chapter 20

Lance and Pat walked around the grounds of Yewtree Lodge. 'There's something extremely frightening about a poisoner,' said Pat. 'I mean they must have a terrible mind, filled with thoughts of revenge.'

'Funny! I just think of it as businesslike and cold-blooded①.'

'To do *three* murders ... Whoever did it *must* be mad,' Pat said.

'Yes,' said Lance, in a low voice. 'I'm afraid so. Please, Pat, go back to London — it worries me to death to have you here.'

Pat said quietly, 'You know who it is, don't you?'

'No, I don't.'

'But you *think* you know ... That's why you're frightened for me. I wish you would tell me. But I'm staying here. Lance, you're my husband and my place is here with you.' She added, 'Although maybe you would be better without me — because I always bring bad luck to the men I love.'

'My dearest, you haven't brought bad luck to me. Look how after I married you, Father sent for me to come home and make friends with him.'

'Yes, and what happened when you did come home? I tell you, I'm unlucky to people.'

Lance took her by the shoulders and shook her. 'You're my Pat and to be married to you is the greatest luck in the world. But Pat, I just wish you'd go away from here.'

---

① cold-blooded *adj.* 冷酷的

'Darling,' said Pat. 'I'm not going.'

'Then when I'm not around, stay close to that old lady. What's-her-name? Marple. Why do you think Aunt Effie asked her to stay here?'

'Goodness knows why Aunt Effie does anything. Lance, how long are *we* going to stay here? The house belongs to your brother now and he doesn't really want us here, does he? Are we going back to East Africa or what?'

'Is that what you'd like to do, Pat?' She nodded.

'That's lucky,' said Lance, 'because it's what I'd like to do, too.'

Pat's face brightened. 'From what you said the other day, I was afraid you might want to stay here.'

'You mustn't say anything about our plans, Pat,' Lance said. 'I want to worry Percival a little longer.'

'Oh, Lance, do be careful.'

'I'll be careful, my sweet, but I don't see why he should always get what *he* wants!'

* * *

With her head a little on one side, Miss Marple sat in the large drawing-room listening to Jennifer Fortescue. Jennifer had a lot of complaints and the relief of telling them to a stranger was huge.

'Of course I never want to complain,' said Jennifer. 'What I always say is that I must put up with things and I'm sure I've never said a word to *anyone*, but in some ways I feel very lonely here. Fortunately our new house is almost ready to move into. My husband, of course, has been quite satisfied living here. But then it's different for a man. Don't you agree?'

Miss Marple agreed, and it was what she really believed. Men needed two eggs plus bacon for breakfast, three good meals a day and were never to be argued with before dinner. Jennifer continued. 'My husband, you see, is away all day in the city. But I am alone here with no pleasant company *at all*. The people round here are really not my kind. They're all very rich down here. They play cards for money, and there's a great deal of drinking. And I don't want to say anything against the dead, but my mother-in-law was absolutely man-mad. And the way she spent money! It troubled Percival very much, very much indeed. And then what with Mr Fortescue being so terribly angry some days and spending huge amounts of money. Well — it wasn't at all nice.'

'That must have worried your husband, too?' asked Miss Marple.

'Oh, yes, it did. For the last year he's been very worried indeed. He changed, even towards me. Then Elaine, my sister-in-law, she's a *very* strange sort of girl. She never wants to go to London and shop, or go to a play. She isn't even interested in clothes.' Jennifer sighed. 'You must think it most strange, talking to you like this when we really don't know one another ...'

'Not at all strange, my dear, I know just how you feel,' said Miss Marple. And this again was true. Jennifer's husband was obviously bored by her and the poor woman hadn't made any local friends. 'I hope it's not rude of me to say so,' said Miss Marple in a gentle old lady's voice, 'but I really feel that Mr Rex Fortescue cannot have been a very nice man.'

'He wasn't,' said his daughter-in-law. 'He was a horrible old man. It's not surprising that someone murdered him.'

'You've no idea at all who ...' began Miss Marple and broke

off. 'Oh dear, perhaps this is a question I should not ask — not even an idea who — who — well, who it might have been?'

'Oh, I think it was that horrible man Crump,' said Jennifer. 'I've always disliked him very much.'

'Still, there would have to be a motive.'

'I really don't know if that sort of person needs much motive. Of course, I *did* suspect that it was *Adele* who poisoned Mr Fortescue. But now we can't suspect that as she's been poisoned herself. Oh dear, sometimes I feel I must get away — that if it doesn't all stop soon, I shall — I shall actually *run away*.' She leant back, studying Miss Marple's face. 'But perhaps — that wouldn't be wise?'

'No — I don't think it would be very wise — the police could soon find you, you know.'

'You think they're clever enough for that?'

'It is very foolish to underestimate① the police. Inspector Neele seems to be a particularly intelligent man,' said Miss Marple.

'I can't help feeling ...' Jennifer Fortescue hesitated, 'that it's dangerous to stay here.'

'Dangerous for you, you mean? Because of something you — know?'

'Oh no — of course I don't know anything. What should I know? It's just — just that I'm nervous. That man Crump ...'

But it was not, Miss Marple thought, of Crump that Mrs Jennifer Fortescue was thinking. And for some reason Jennifer Fortescue was very badly frightened indeed.

---

① underestimate *v.* 低估

Chapter 21

It was getting dark. Miss Marple had taken her knitting① over to the glass doors in the library. Looking out she saw Pat Fortescue walking up and down outside. Miss Marple opened the door and called, 'Come in, my dear. It's much too damp for you to be out there without a coat on.'

Pat came in and closed the door behind her and turned on two of the lamps. 'Yes,' she said, 'it's not a very nice afternoon.' She sat down on the sofa by Miss Marple. 'What are you making?'

'Oh, just a little baby's coat, dear. I always make the second size. Babies so soon grow out of the first size.'

Pat stretched out long legs towards the fire. 'It's nice in here today,' she said. 'With the fire and the lamps and you knitting things for babies. It all seems just like England *ought* to be.'

'It's like England *is*,' said Miss Marple. 'There are not so many Yewtree Lodges, my dear.'

'I don't believe anybody was ever happy here, in spite of all the money and the things they had. Oh, *how* I want to get away from here!' She looked at Miss Marple and smiled suddenly. 'Do you know, Lance told me to stay as close to you as I could. He seemed to think I would be safe that way.'

'Your husband's no fool,' said Miss Marple.

'No. Somebody in this house is mad, and madness is always frightening, because you don't know how mad people's minds will work. You don't know what they'll do next.'

---

① knitting *n.* 针织品

'My poor child,' said Miss Marple.

'Oh, I'm all right, really. I ought to be tough enough by now.'

Miss Marple said gently, 'You've had a lot of unhappiness, haven't you, my dear?'

'Oh, I've had some very good times, too. I had a lovely childhood in Ireland, riding horses, swimming in the sea when the weather was good ... It was afterwards — when I grew up — that things seemed always to go wrong.'

'Your first husband was a pilot in the war, wasn't he?'

'Yes. We had only been married about a month when Don's plane was shot down. I thought at first I wanted to die, too. And yet — in the end — I almost began to see that it had been the best thing. Don was brave and reckless — all the qualities that are needed in a war. But I don't believe peace would have suited him. He would have fought against things. He was — well, anti-social① in a way. No, he wouldn't have fitted in.'

'It's wise of you to see that, my dear. And your second husband?'

'Freddy? We were very happy together, but Freddy wasn't very honest in his horse-racing business. However, it didn't seem to matter, between us two, that is. Because, you see, Freddy loved me and I loved him and I tried not to know what was happening. That wasn't very brave, I suppose, but I couldn't have changed him you know. You can't change people.'

'No,' said Miss Marple, 'you can't change people.'

'Then things went wrong and he shot himself and I went out to Kenya to stay with some friends there. And I met Lance.'

---

① anti-social *adj.* 反社会的

Her face softened, then after a short pause she said, 'Tell me, Miss Marple, what do *you* really think of Percival?'

'Well, I don't think he likes my being here very much.'

Pat laughed suddenly. 'He's mean. He goes over the housekeeping accounts with Miss Dove, complaining about every item. But Miss Dove manages to win every time. She's really rather wonderful, don't you think?'

'Yes, indeed,' agreed Miss Marple. 'She reminds me of Mrs Latimer in my own village, St Mary Mead. She ran the Girl Guides, and indeed, she ran practically everything there. She had been doing it for five years when we discovered that ... oh, but I mustn't gossip. You must forgive me, my dear.'

'Is St Mary Mead a very nice village?'

'Well, it's quite a *pretty* village. There are some nice people living in it and some extremely unpleasant people as well. Human nature is much the same everywhere, is it not?'

'You go up and see Miss Ramsbottom a lot, don't you?' said Pat. 'Now she *really* frightens me. She sits up there and thinks about wickedness. Well, she might have felt in the end that it was up to her to deliver justice[①].'

'Is that what your husband thinks?'

'I don't know *what* Lance thinks about the murders really. But I'm quite sure of one thing — that he believes that the murderer is someone who's mad, and it's someone in the family. And I don't see how it can be anybody from outside. And so — and so that's why there's this terrible atmosphere here. Everyone is watching everybody else. Only something's got to happen soon.'

'There won't be any more deaths,' said Miss Marple. 'The

---

① justice n. 正义

murderer's got what he or she wanted, you see.'

'And what is that?'

Miss Marple shook her head — she was not yet quite sure herself.

Chapter 22

In the office of *Consolidated Investments*, once again Miss Somers had just made tea in the typists' room, and once again the kettle had not been boiling. As so often before, Miss Griffith said sharply, 'The water's not boiling *again*, Somers,' but she was interrupted by the entrance of Lance Fortescue. Miss Griffith jumped up. 'Mr Lance,' she exclaimed.

His face lit up in a smile. 'Hello, Miss Griffith.'

Miss Griffith was delighted. Eleven years since he had seen her and he knew her name. She said in an excited voice, 'You remember me!'

And Lance said easily, smiling his attractive smile, 'Of course I remember.' He looked round him. 'So everything's still going on just the same here.'

'Not many changes, Mr Lance. I suppose you must have had a very interesting life abroad.'

'You could call it that,' said Lance, 'but perhaps I am now going to try and have an interesting life in London.'

'You're coming back here to the office?'

'Maybe. You'll have to show me how everything works again, Miss Griffith.'

Miss Griffith laughed delightedly. 'It will be very nice to have you back, Mr Lance. Very nice indeed. We never believed — none of us thought ...' Miss Griffith broke off.

Lance patted her on the arm. 'You didn't believe I was as guilty as it seemed I was? Well, perhaps I wasn't. But that's all old history now. The future's the important thing now.' He added, 'Is my brother here?'

'He's in the inner office.'

Lance nodded and walked on through to his father's office. Somewhat to his surprise it was not Percival who was sitting behind the desk there, but Inspector Neele.

'Good morning, Mr Fortescue. Are you really going to become a city man①? It doesn't seem the kind of life that would suit you.'

Lance sat down, smiling. 'You're more intelligent than my brother, Inspector. Percival thinks I've decided to join the firm again and that I'll spend the firm's money on risky investments. It would be almost worth doing just for the fun of it! But I couldn't really stand an office life. However, I want to make him worry a bit. I've got to have just a little revenge!'

'There was a problem with a forged cheque some years ago, I understand. Would that be what you want revenge for?' enquired Inspector Neele.

'How much you know, Inspector!'

'There was no question of prosecution, I understand,' said Neele. 'Your father wouldn't have done that.'

'No. He just got rid of② me, that's all.'

Inspector Neele thought about Percival. It seemed to him that wherever his investigations got in the case, there was Percival Fortescue. On the surface, he seemed to be a man who had never said no to his father. Neele was trying now, through Lance, to learn more about Percival's personality. 'Your brother seems always to have been very much — well, how shall I put it — controlled by your father.'

'I don't know,' Lance said. 'I'm not sure that it was really the truth. It's amazing, when I look back through life, to see

---

① city man *n*. 金融机构雇员　② get rid of 除掉

how Percival always got what he wanted without seeming to do so, if you know what I mean.'

Neele pushed a letter across the desk towards Lance. 'This is a letter you wrote last August, isn't it, Mr Fortescue?'

'Yes,' he said, 'I wrote it after I got back to Kenya last summer, saying I would rejoin the firm. Where was it — here in the office?'

'No, it was among your father's papers in Yewtree Lodge. Where did you address this letter, Mr Fortescue?'

Lance frowned. 'The office. Why?'

'I wondered,' said Inspector Neele. 'Your father did not put it on the file here among his private papers. I found it in his desk at Yewtree Lodge there. I wondered why he would have done that.'

Lance laughed. 'To hide it from Percival, I suppose. He always did read other people's letters. And just look who's here!'

Percival Fortescue came in. About to speak to the Inspector he stopped, frowning, as he saw Lance. 'Hello,' he said. 'You didn't tell me you were coming here today.'

'Oh, I felt I had to come and get started on my new working life,' said Lance. 'By the way, why did you get rid of the old man's glamorous secretary, Grosvenor? Did you think she knew a bit too much?'

'Of course not. What an idea!' Percy spoke angrily. He turned to the Inspector. 'You mustn't pay any attention to my brother,' he said coldly. 'He has a rather strange sense of humour. I never had a very high opinion of Miss Grosvenor's intelligence and in any case, we have to save money — the firm is in a bad state.'

'That's one of the things I wanted to talk to you about, Mr Fortescue,' Inspector Neele said to Percival.

'Yes, Inspector?'

'I understand that your father's recent behaviour made you worry and you tried to make him see a doctor, but he refused?'

'That is correct.'

'May I ask you if you suspected that your father had one of those mental illnesses which make people behave in an extreme way?'

'That is exactly what I *did* suspect.'

Neele continued, 'So from the business point of view, your father's death was very fortunate.'

'You can't believe that I would think of my father's death in that way!'

'It is not a question of how you think of it, Mr Fortescue. I'm speaking about a fact.'

'Yes. But really, Inspector, I don't see what you're trying to say ...' Percival broke off.

'Oh, I'm not trying to say anything, Mr Fortescue,' said Neele. 'I just like getting my facts together. Now, you said that you hadn't had any communication at all with your brother since he left England many years ago — but last spring you wrote and told him you were worried about your father's behaviour. You wanted your brother to support you in getting your father medically examined.'

'I — I — I thought it only right. After all, Lance was a junior partner.'

Inspector Neele looked at Lance, who was smiling.

'You received that letter?' Inspector Neele asked.

Lance Fortescue nodded.

'What did you reply to it?'

'I told Percy to leave the old man alone. I said the old man knew what he was doing. And that is one of the reasons why, when I got a letter from my father, I came home to see for myself. In the short interview I had with my father, he appeared to me to be quite capable of managing his business. Anyway, after I got back to Africa and had talked things over with Pat, I decided that I would come home and make sure that my father wasn't pushed into something that he didn't want.' He looked at Percival as he spoke.

'I object strongly to what you are suggesting. I was worried about my father's health. I admit that I was also worried ...' Percival paused.

Lance filled the pause quickly. 'Worried about your pocket, eh?' He got up and all of a sudden his behaviour changed. 'All right, Percy, I was going to annoy you for a while by pretending to work here, but I've had enough of it. It makes me sick to be in the same room with you. You've always been nasty and mean since you were a child, lying and making trouble. I've always believed it was *you* who forged that cheque — for one thing it was a very bad forgery. I can't understand why Father didn't realize that if *I had* forged his name, I would have done it much better. Well, I'm sick of little men like you with their almost criminal financial deals. We'll divide everything as you suggested, and I'll get back with Pat to a country where there's room to breathe. Give me Father's latest risky investments. I'll bet that one or two of them will make a great deal of money in the end! As for you, you little ...' Lance walked towards his brother, who stepped backwards quickly.

'All right,' said Lance, 'I'm not going to touch you. You wanted me out of here, you're getting me out of here.' He added as he walked towards the door, 'You can also give me the old Blackbird Mine too, if you like. If we've got murdering MacKenzies following us, I'll lead them off to Africa. Revenge — after all these years — it doesn't seem likely. But Inspector Neele seems to take it seriously, don't you, Inspector?'

'Nonsense,' said Percival. 'Such a thing is impossible!'

Gently stroking his upper lip, Inspector Neele said, 'You remember the blackbirds last summer, Mr Fortescue. There *are* reasons for us to investigate.'

'Nonsense,' said Percival again. 'Nobody's heard of the MacKenzies for years.'

'And yet,' said Lance, 'I'd almost believe that there's a MacKenzie very near us. I imagine the Inspector thinks so, too.'

* * *

Inspector Neele followed Lance Fortescue into the street. 'Mr Fortescue, when you came into the inner office and saw me, you were surprised. Why?'

'Because I thought I'd find Percy there. Miss Griffith said he was in his office.'

'I see — so nobody knew he'd gone out. There's no second door out of the inner office — but there is a door leading straight into the corridor from the secretary's office — I suppose your brother went out that way.'

Lance looked at him. 'What's the idea, Inspector?'

'Just puzzling over a few little things, that's all, Mr Fortescue.'

Chapter 23

On the train on the way back down to Baydon Heath, Inspector Neele read the news in *The Times* with only half his brain taking it in. He read of an earthquake in Japan; of the discovery in Tanganyika of valuable uranium①, needed to make nuclear weapons; of the body of a sailor found on the beach near Southampton. All these items made a strange kind of pattern in the back of his mind and when he reached Yewtree Lodge he had made a decision. He said to Sergeant Hay, 'Where's Miss Marple? I'd like to see her.'

Miss Marple arrived a few minutes later, looking quite pink. 'You want to see me, Inspector Neele? I do hope I haven't kept you waiting. I was in the kitchen talking to Mrs Crump about her wonderful cooking.'

'What you really wanted to talk to her about,' said Inspector Neele, 'was Gladys Martin?'

Miss Marple nodded. 'Yes. Gladys. You see, Mrs Crump was able to tell me about her behaviour lately and the things she said. I really think, you know, that things are becoming very much clearer, don't you?'

'I do and I don't. Look here, Miss Marple, I've heard something about you at the Yard.' He smiled, 'It seems you're fairly well known there.'

'I don't know how it is,' said Miss Marple, 'but I so often seem to get mixed up in crimes and strange events.'

'You've got a reputation②,' said Inspector Neele, 'and you

---

① uranium *n.* 铀 ② reputation *n.* 名声

and I have different points of view. But our base is the same. This murder benefits certain people. One person in particular. The second murder benefits the same person. But the third murder — well, you could say the third murder was done to keep the murderer safe.'

'But which do you call the *third* murder?' Miss Marple asked. Her eyes, a very bright blue, looked intelligently at the Inspector. He nodded. 'Yes. When the Assistant Comissioner was speaking to me of these murders, something that he said seemed to me to be wrong. That was it. The nursery rhyme says: the king in his counting house, the queen in the parlour and the maid hanging out the clothes.'

'Exactly,' said Miss Marple. 'But actually Gladys must have been murdered *before* Mrs Fortescue, mustn't she?'

'I think so,' said Neele. 'Her body wasn't discovered till late that night, but she must almost certainly have been murdered round about five o'clock, because otherwise she would have taken the second tray into the drawing room. She took one tray in with the tea on it, and then she saw or heard something. It *might* have been Dubois coming down the stairs from Mrs Fortescue's room. It *might* have been Gerald Wright coming in at the side door. Whoever it was persuaded① her to leave the tea tray and go out into the garden. And once that had happened I believe she was killed immediately.'

'You're quite right,' said Miss Marple. 'It was never a case of "the maid was in the garden hanging up the clothes". She wouldn't be hanging up clothes at that time of the evening and the clothes peg was simply to make the thing fit in with the rhyme.'

---

① persuade *v.* 劝说

'It fits,' said Neele, 'but I'm going to describe *my* side of the case now, Miss Marple. I'm going by the simple facts and the reasons for which sane people do murders. First, the death of Rex Fortescue, and *who benefits by his death*. Well, most of all, Percival. If a hundred thousand pounds had to be paid to Adele Fortescue according to her husband's will, *Consolidated* would have been finished as a business. But she didn't live longer than a month after her husband's death and the person who gained from her death was Percival Fortescue again. But although he *could* have put the taxine into the marmalade, he couldn't have poisoned his stepmother or strangled Gladys. According to his secretary he was in his city office at five o'clock that afternoon, and he didn't arrive back here until nearly seven. However, there are other people who had a perfectly good motive.'

'Mr Dubois, of course,' said Miss Marple. 'And that young Mr Wright. Whenever there is any question of *gain*, one has to be *very suspicious*. Never trust anyone.'

Neele smiled. Miss Marple never failed to surprise him! 'Always think the worst, eh?' he asked.

'Oh yes,' said Miss Marple. 'Always!'

'All right,' said Neele, 'let's think the worst. Dubois could have done it, Gerald Wright could have done it if he had been working together with Elaine Fortescue and she put the taxine in the marmalade. Jennifer Fortescue could have done it, but none of them seem to have any connection with blackbirds and pockets full of rye. That's *your* theory① and it points to one person. Mrs MacKenzie's in a mental hospital and her son Donald was killed in the war. That leaves the daughter, Ruby

---

① theory *n*. 推测

MacKenzie. And if *your* theory is correct, if this whole series of murders is because of the old Blackbird Mine business, then Ruby MacKenzie must be here in this house, and there's only one person that Ruby MacKenzie could be.'

'I think, you know,' said Miss Marple, 'that you may not be seeing the whole picture, Inspector.'

Inspector Neele paid no attention. 'Just one person,' he said. He got up and went out of the room.

* * *

Mary Dove was in her sitting room. How wonderfully self-controlled the girl was, Neele thought. She said calmly, 'Yes, Inspector? What can I do for you?'

Inspector Neele said quietly, 'Is your real name Dove?'

Mary raised her eyebrows. 'Are you suggesting that my name is *not* Mary Dove?'

'I'm suggesting that your name is Ruby MacKenzie. *Is* your name Ruby MacKenzie?'

'I have told you my name is Mary Dove. Do you want to see my birth certificate①?'

'You might *have* the birth certificate of *a* Mary Dove. That Mary Dove might be a friend of yours or might be someone who had died.'

'Yes, there are a lot of possibilities, aren't there?' There was laughter now in Mary Dove's voice. 'I think you know, Inspector, that you have to prove I *am* this Ruby MacKenzie, whoever she is.' Looking him straight in the eyes, Mary Dove said, 'Yes, Inspector. Prove that I'm Ruby MacKenzie, if you can.'

---

① birth certificate *n*. 出生证明

Chapter 24

Miss Marple was talking to Jennifer Fortescue while she knitted. 'I had such a nice nurse looking after me when I once broke my wrist. She went on from me to nurse Mrs Sparrow's son, a very nice young naval officer and they married and had two dear little children. That was the beginning of *your* romance, was it not? I mean, you came here to nurse Mr Percival Fortescue, did you not? One should not listen to servants' gossip, of course, but I'm afraid an old lady like myself is always interested to hear about the people in the house. There was another nurse at first, was there not, and she got sent away — something like that? They said she was careless, I believe.'

'I don't think she was careless,' said Jennifer. 'I believe her father was extremely ill, and so I came to replace her.'

'I see,' said Miss Marple. 'And you fell in love with Percival and that was that. Yes, very nice indeed, very nice.'

'I'm not so sure about that,' said Jennifer Fortescue. 'I often wish ...' her voice was very quiet, 'I was back in the hospital again. Life's so boring, you know. Oh, it's what I deserve! I should not have done it.'

'Should not have done what, my dear?'

'I should not have married Percival. Oh, well,' she sighed. 'Don't let's talk of it any more.'

And Miss Marple began to talk about the new skirts that were being worn in Paris.

* * *

Miss Marple knocked at the door of the study and Inspector Neele told her to come in.

'We didn't really finish our talk just now,' she said, 'and I wasn't quite ready then to make any accusation unless I was absolutely sure about it. And I *am* sure, now.'

'You're sure about what, Miss Marple?'

'Well, certainly about who killed Mr Fortescue. The marmalade shows *how*, as well as *who*, and though she was not clever, she was intelligent enough to do it. The beginning is Gladys. And what with the nylon stockings and the telephone calls and one thing and another, it was perfectly clear as to who put the taxine into Mr Fortescue's marmalade.'

'You have a theory?' asked Inspector Neele.

'It isn't a theory,' said Miss Marple. 'I *know*.'

Inspector Neele looked surprised.

'It was Gladys, of course,' said Miss Marple.

Chapter 25

'Are you saying,' Inspector Neele said, astonished, 'that *Gladys Martin* deliberately murdered Rex Fortescue?'

'No, of course she didn't *mean* to murder him,' said Miss Marple, 'but she put the taxine in the marmalade. She didn't think it was poison, of course.'

'What *did* she think it was?'

'I believe she thought it was a truth drug,' said Miss Marple. 'It's very interesting, you know, the things these girls cut out of papers and keep, because they believe that if a story is in a newspaper, then it must be true. And if she had it read in the papers, then Gladys would have believed it when he told her that it was a truth drug.'

'When who told her?' said Inspector Neele.

'Albert Evans,' said Miss Marple. 'That's not his *real* name, of course. He met her last summer at a holiday camp, and he said sweet things to her, kissed her, and probably told her some story of being cheated out of money by Rex Fortescue. The point was that Rex Fortescue had to be made to confess what he had done. I don't *know* this, of course, Inspector Neele, but I'm quite sure about it. He persuaded her to take a job here — it's really very easy nowadays with the shortage of domestic staff, to get a job where you want one. They then arranged a date together. You remember on that last postcard he said, *Remember our date*. That was to be the day Gladys would put the drug that he gave her into the top of the marmalade, so that Mr Fortescue would eat it at breakfast, and she would also put the rye in his pocket. I don't know what story he told her to explain the rye, but Gladys Martin was a girl who would believe almost anything.'

'Please continue,' said Inspector Neele in an amazed voice.

'The idea probably was that Albert was going to visit him at the office that day, and that by that time the truth drug would have worked, and so Mr Fortescue would confess everything. You can imagine the poor girl's feelings when she heard that Mr Fortescue was dead.'

'But, surely,' Inspector Neele objected, 'she would have told someone?'

'What was the first thing she said to you when you questioned her?'

'She said, "I didn't do it,"' Inspector Neele said.

'Exactly,' said Miss Marple. 'When she worked for me, Gladys would always say if she broke anything, "I didn't do it, Miss Marple. I can't think *how* it happened." You don't think that a nervous young woman who had murdered someone when she didn't mean to murder him, is going to admit it, do you? Her first idea would be to deny it all. Then in a confused way she would try to sort it all out. Perhaps Albert hadn't known how strong the truth drug was. She'd think of excuses for him. She would hope he would contact her, which he did. By telephone. There were unexplained calls that day. People rang up and, when Crump or Mrs Crump answered, nobody spoke, so they would put the telephone down. That's what he would do, you know. Ring up and wait until Gladys answered the phone, and then he would make an appointment with her to meet him.'

'You mean she had an appointment to meet him on the day she died.'

Miss Marple nodded quickly. 'Yes. The girl was wearing her

best nylon stockings and her good shoes. Only she wasn't going *out* to meet him. He was coming to Yewtree Lodge. That's why she was so excited and late with tea. Then, as she brought the second tray into the hall, she looked along the hall to the side door, and saw him there, waving to her. She put the tray down and went out to meet him.'

'And then he strangled her,' said Neele.

'He couldn't risk her talking. She had to die, poor, silly girl. And then — he put a clothes peg on her nose!' There was great anger in the old lady's voice. 'To make it fit in with the rhyme. The rye, the blackbirds, the counting house, the bread and honey, and the clothes peg — the nearest he could get to a little dickey bird that nipped off her nose —'

'And I suppose at the end of it all he'll go to Broadmoor① and we won't be able to hang② him because he's crazy!' said Neele slowly.

'I think you'll hang him all right,' said Miss Marple. 'He's not crazy, Inspector!'

Inspector Neele looked hard at her. 'Now see here, Miss Marple, you're saying that a man is responsible for these crimes. A man who called himself Albert Evans was someone who wanted revenge for the old Blackbird Mine business. You're suggesting, aren't you, that Mrs MacKenzie's son, Don MacKenzie, didn't die in France. That he is responsible for all this?'

'Oh no!' she said. 'This blackbird business is a complete *fake*. It was *used*, that was all, by somebody who heard about the blackbirds on the desk and in the pie. The blackbirds were real enough. They were put there by someone who knew about

---

① Broadmoor *n*. 布罗德莫精神病院 ② hang *v*. 绞死

the old business, who wanted revenge for it. But only the revenge of trying to frighten Mr Fortescue. I don't believe that children can really be brought up to carry out revenge. But someone whose father had been cheated and perhaps left to die, might want to play a trick on the person who was supposed to have done it. That's what happened, I think. And the killer used it.'

'The killer,' said Inspector Neele. 'Who was he?'

'He's sane, brilliantly intelligent, and quite without morals[①]. And he did it, of course, for money.'

'Percival Fortescue?' Inspector Neele almost begged, but he knew as he spoke that he was wrong.

'Oh, no,' said Miss Marple. 'Not Percival. Lance.'

---

① morals *n.* 道德

Chapter 26

Miss Marple leaned forward in her chair. 'He's always been bad, completely bad, although he's also always been *attractive*. Especially attractive to *women*. And because of his charm, people have always believed the best about him. He came home in the summer to see his father. I don't believe for a moment that his father invited him — he probably flew over here and tried to get his father to forgive him, but Mr Fortescue wouldn't do it. You see, Lance was very much in love with Pat — who is a dear girl — and he wanted a respectable life with her. And that meant having a lot of money.

'When he was at Yewtree Lodge, he must have heard about these blackbirds. He guessed that MacKenzie's daughter was in the house and he realized that she would make a very good scapegoat① for murder. Because when he couldn't get his father to do what he wanted, he cold-bloodedly decided that murder it would have to be. Perhaps the coincidence② of his father's first name being *Rex*, together with hearing about the blackbirds in the pie, suggested the idea of the nursery rhyme. Then he could make a crazy business of the whole thing — and connect it to that old revenge threat of the MacKenzies. Then, you see, he could kill Adele, too, and stop that hundred thousand pounds going out of the firm. But there would have to be a third character, the "maid in the garden hanging up the clothes". An innocent accomplice③ whom he could silence before she could

---

① scapegoat *n*. 替罪羊 ② coincidence *n*. 巧合 ③ accomplice *n*. 同谋

talk. And that would give him a real alibi① for the first murder.

'He arrived here just before five o'clock, which was the time Gladys brought the second tray into the hall. He came to the side door and waved to her. It would only have taken him three or four minutes to strangle her and carry her body to where the clothes lines were. Then he rang the front-door bell and joined the family for tea. After tea he went up to see Miss Ramsbottom. When he came down, he went into the drawing room, found Adele alone, drinking a last cup of tea, and sat down by her on the sofa. While he was talking to her, he managed to put the cyanide into her tea without her noticing.'

Inspector Neele said slowly, 'But I cannot see what he thought he would get from it. Of course, unless old Fortescue died, the business would soon be finished, but is Lance's share really big enough to make him plan three murders?'

'That *is* a little difficult,' admitted Miss Marple. 'But is it really true that the Blackbird Mine *is* worthless?'

Neele thought about it. A gold mine. A worthless gold mine. And where *was* the mine? West Africa, Lance had said. But Miss Ramsbottom had said it was in *East* Africa. Lance had just come from East Africa. Maybe he had some recent knowledge?

Suddenly another piece fitted into the Inspector's puzzle. Sitting in the train, reading *The Times*. *Uranium deposits found in Tanganyika*. What if the uranium was in the Blackbird Mine? Lance was there when it was found — and knew the mine was now worth a fortune. An *enormous* fortune! Neele sighed and looked at Miss Marple. 'How do you think,' he asked, 'that I'm ever going to be able to prove all this?'

Miss Marple nodded at him encouragingly. 'You'll prove

---

① alibi *n*. 不在犯罪现场证明

it,' she said. 'You're a very, *very* clever man, Inspector Neele. Now you know who it is, you ought to be able to get the evidence. At that holiday camp they'll recognize Lance's photograph. He must have gone there when he came over to see his father, looking for an innocent, vulnerable① girl who would do anything for him. He'll find it hard to explain why he stayed there for a week, calling himself Albert Evans.'

'Yes,' Inspector Neele thought, 'I'll get him!' Then, suddenly feeling unsure, he looked at Miss Marple. 'It's all theory, you know.'

'Yes — but you are sure, aren't you?'

'I suppose so. After all, I've known people like him before.'

The old lady nodded. 'Yes — that's really why *I'm* sure.'

'Because of your knowledge of criminals?' Neele asked.

'Oh no — of course not. Because of Pat — a dear girl — and the kind that always marries a bad man — that's really what made me suspect him at the start.'

'But there's a lot that needs explaining,' said the Inspector. 'The Ruby MacKenzie business for instance. I could swear that ...'

Miss Marple interrupted, 'Go and talk to Jennifer.'

* * *

'Mrs Fortescue,' said Inspector Neele, 'do you mind telling me your name before you were married.'

'Oh!' Jennifer exclaimed. 'It — it was MacKenzie ...'

'You needn't be nervous, Madam,' said Inspector Neele gently, and added, 'I was talking to your mother a few days

---

① vulnerable *adj.* 脆弱的

ago at *Pinewood Sanatorium.*'

'She's very angry with me,' said Jennifer. 'Poor Mother, she loved Dad so much. She kept making us promise that we would kill Rex Fortescue one day. Of course, once I'd started my nursing training, I began to realize that her mental balance wasn't what it should be.'

'You yourself must have wanted revenge though, Mrs Fortescue?'

'Well, of course I did. Rex Fortescue practically murdered my father! I'm quite certain that he left Father to die. So I did want to pay him back. When a friend of mine came to nurse his son, Percival, I persuaded her to leave and suggested that I replace her. I don't know exactly what I meant to do. I had some idea, I think, of nursing his son so badly that he would die. But of course, if you *are* a nurse, you can't do that sort of thing. Actually I had great difficulty saving Percival. And then he asked me to marry him and I thought, "Well, that's a far more sensible revenge than anything else." I mean, to marry Mr Fortescue's eldest son and get the money he cheated Father out of that way.'

'Yes, indeed,' said Inspector Neele, 'far more sensible. It was you, I suppose, who put the blackbirds on the desk and in the pie?'

Jennifer looked down. 'Yes. I suppose it was silly of me really ... But I didn't do anything *else*! You don't — you don't honestly think I would *murder* anyone, do you?'

Inspector Neele smiled. 'No,' he said, 'I don't.' He added, 'By the way, have you given Miss Dove any money lately?'

Jennifer looked shocked. 'How did you know?'

'We know a lot of things,' said Inspector Neele and added to himself: And guess a good many, too.

'She came to me and said that you had accused her of being Ruby MacKenzie. She said if I gave her five hundred pounds, she would let you continue thinking she was Ruby MacKenzie. I found it very difficult to get the money. I had to sell a very beautiful necklace my husband had given me.'

'Don't worry, Mrs Fortescue,' said Inspector Neele, 'I think we can get your money back for you.'

* * *

Inspector Neele had another interview with Miss Mary Dove. 'I wonder, Miss Dove,' he said, 'if you would give me a cheque for five hundred pounds payable to Mrs Jennifer Fortescue.' He had the pleasure of seeing Mary Dove's calmness disappear.

'The silly fool told you, I suppose,' she said.

'Yes. Blackmail①, Miss Dove, is rather a serious crime.'

'I think you'd find it hard to prove that I was guilty of blackmail.'

'Well, if you'll give me that cheque, Miss Dove, we'll leave it like that. Otherwise we have no proof against you at all. It is a strange, though, that in each of the last three places you have worked, there have been robberies about three months after you left. The thieves seemed to have known exactly where fur coats, jewels, etc. were kept. Strange coincidence, isn't it?'

'Coincidences do happen, Inspector.'

'Oh, yes,' said Neele. 'But they mustn't happen too often, Miss Dove. It is possible,' he added, 'that we may meet again in the future.'

---

① blackmail n. 敲诈

'I hope ...' said Mary Dove, 'I don't mean to be rude, Inspector Neele — but I hope we don't.'

Chapter 27

Miss Marple went to say goodbye to Miss Ramsbottom. 'I'm afraid,' said Miss Marple, 'that I've repaid you badly for your kindness to me.'

'Hah,' said Miss Ramsbottom. 'You found out what you wanted to, I suppose. And I suppose you've told that police Inspector all about it? Will he be able to prove a case?'

'I'm almost sure he will,' said Miss Marple. 'It may take a little time.'

'I don't blame you for what you've done. Wickedness is wickedness and has got to be punished. Handsome, Lance is, but he has always been bad. Yes, I was afraid of it. Ah, well, sometimes it can be difficult not to love a bad boy. The boy always had charm. He lied about the time he left me that day Adele died. But he was my beloved sister Elvira's boy — I couldn't possibly say anything against him. You're a good woman, Jane Marple, and good must always win. I'm sorry for his wife, though.'

'So am I,' said Miss Marple.

* * *

In the hall Pat Fortescue was waiting to say goodbye. 'I wish you weren't going,' she said. 'I shall miss you.'

'It's time for me to go,' said Miss Marple. 'I've finished what I came here to do. It's important, you know, that wickedness shouldn't win.'

Pat looked puzzled. 'I don't understand.'

'No, my dear. But if I might advise you, if anything ever goes wrong in your life — go back to where you were happy as a child. Go back to Ireland, my dear. Horses and dogs. All that.'

Pat nodded. 'Sometimes I wish I had done just that when Freddy died. But if I had,' her voice softened, 'I would not have met Lance. We're not staying here, you know. We're going back to East Africa. I'm so pleased.'

'Be happy, dear child,' said Miss Marple. 'One needs a great deal of courage to get through life. I think you have it.' She patted the girl's hand and went through the front door to the waiting taxi.

* * *

Miss Marple reached home late that evening. Kitty — the latest girl she had taken in to train — greeted her with a smiling face. 'I'm so happy to see you — you'll find everything very nice in the house. I've cleaned and cleaned!'

'That's very nice, Kitty — I'm happy to be home.' There were six spider's webs on the ceiling, Miss Marple noted. These girls never looked up. She was too kind to say anything.

'Your letters are on the hall table, Miss. And there's one that was delivered to the wrong house — it only arrived today.'

Miss Marple recognized the childish handwriting. She tore the envelope open.

Dear Madam,

I hope you'll forgive me writing this but I really don't know what to do and I never meant any harm. It was murder, they say, but it wasn't me that did it, not really. I would never do anything wicked like that and I know he wouldn't either. Albert, I mean.

We met last summer and we were going to be married, but Albert *had been cheated out of his inheritance*① *by Mr Rex Fortescue. And Mr Fortescue just denied everything and everybody believed him, and not Albert, because he was rich and Albert was poor. But Albert has a friend who works in a place where they make these new drugs and they have what they call a truth drug and it makes people speak the truth whether they want to or not.*

Albert was going to see Mr Fortescue in his office on Nov. 5th, taking a lawyer with him. The only thing I had to do was to give Mr Fortescue the drug at breakfast that morning and then it would work just when they arrived and he'd admit that everything that Albert said was quite true. Well, Madam, I put the drug in the marmalade — but now Mr Fortescue is dead! I think it must have been too strong, but it wasn't Albert's fault because Albert would never do a thing like that. I can't tell the police because maybe they'd think Albert did it on purpose, which I know he didn't.

Oh, Madam, I don't know what to do and I haven't heard from Albert. If you could only come here and help me, they'd listen to you. You were always so kind to me, and I didn't mean to do anything wrong and Albert didn't either. If you could only help us. Yours respectfully,

Gladys Martin.

P. S. — I'm enclosing a photograph of Albert and me. One of the boys took it at the holiday camp and gave it to me. Albert doesn't know I've got it — he hates being photographed. But you can see, Madam, what a nice boy he is.

Miss Marple stared down at the photograph, to the dark, handsome, smiling face of Lance Fortescue. The last words of

---

① inheritance *n.* 遗产

the sad little letter echoed in her mind, *You can see what a nice boy he is.*

Tears rose in Miss Marple's eyes. But following her sadness for poor Gladys, there came anger — anger against a cold-blooded killer.

And then there came a huge feeling of triumph① — there was no escape now for Lance Fortescue!

---

① triumph *n.* 胜利

文化注释

Stocks, shares and investments

The Fortescue's family firm was one that did business by using money to make more money in the world of finance. They bought and sold stocks and shares on the stock exchange and invested in companies and other businesses in the hope that they would become more successful and make a profit. Rex Fortescue had bought *Blackbird Mine* when he was a young man in the hope that it would produce a lot of gold and is one of the investments that Percival thinks was foolish and risky.

股票、证券与投资

Fortescue 家族企业的业务就是在金融世界中以钱生钱。他们在证券交易所中买卖股票和证券,并在其他公司和业务中投资,期望通过其优异的表现获取利润。Rex Fortescue 年轻时买下了乌鸫矿(Blackbird Mine),希望可以出产大量的黄金,但 Percival 认为这笔投资十分愚蠢,而且风险过高。

The structure of the Police in England

The structure of the police force in Britain is as follows: the ranks, starting at the lowest, are: Police Constable, Sergeant, Inspector, Chief Inspector, Superintendent, Chief Superintendent. In *A Pocket Full of Rye*, Neele has the rank of Detective Inspector which means that he was a member of either the Special Branch or the CID (Criminal Investigations Department), which trained policemen to deal with all kinds of criminal investigations, including murder. Detectives do not usually wear uniform. Hay, who is a sergeant, is junior to Neele.

The Assistant Commissioner is the third highest police officer in the Metropolitan Police. *Scotland Yard* is actually the name of the head office of the Metropolitan Police. It is in London.

英格兰的警察组织结构

英国的警察组织结构如下,级别从低到高分别为警员、警长、督察、高级督察、警司、高级警司。在《黑麦奇案》中,Neele 的警衔为督察,这意味着他是政治保安处(Special Branch)或者刑事调查局(Criminal Investigations Department,简称 CID)的成员,后者训练警员进行各种罪案调查,包括凶杀案。探员并不总穿着制服。Hay 为警长,是 Neele 的下级。

高级督察是伦敦警察厅(Metropolitan Police)内第三高的级别。"苏格兰场"实际是伦敦警察厅总部的名称,位于伦敦。

Autopsies and inquests

In the UK, when a person dies, the cause of death has to be officially certified by a doctor. If the doctor does not know why the person died — for example if the death was sudden or suspicious — they ask for an autopsy. This is a medical examination to find out the cause of death, and is usually done by an expert doctor called a pathologist, who removes the internal organs of the dead person and examines them.

In cases of sudden, violent or suspicious death, it is common to hold a public inquiry called an inquest to find out why the person died. The coroner is the person in charge of the inquest, and the official cause of death is decided by a jury of twelve ordinary people chosen from the local community.

At the inquest, the coroner and the jury hears medical evidence, as well as evidence from any other people that may be relevant. The family of the person who died and members of the public can also attend the inquest.

Once all the evidence has been heard, the jury gives its verdict — for example natural death (e.g. a heart attack), accidental death, suicide or murder.

尸检和死因审理

在英国,一个人死亡时,其死因必须由医生出具官方证明。如果医生没有搞清死者的死因——例如事件发生得十分突然或者可疑——便会要求尸检。这是一种旨在查明死因的医学检查,通常由称为"病理学家"(pathologist)的医疗专家完成,他们会取出死者体内的器官并进行化验。

发生突然、暴力或可疑的命案时,通常要进行公开的调查,这称为"死因审理",目的是查明遇害者的死因。验尸官是负责死因审理的人,而官方公布的死因则由12人陪审团裁决,其成员均是从当地社区选出的普通人。

进行死因审理时,验尸官和陪审团听取医生提供的证言,同时还有其他相关人士的证词。受害者的家人和公众也可以参加死因审理。

一旦听取完全部证言,陪审团会做出裁决——例如:自然死亡(如心脏病)、意外死亡、自杀或谋杀。

Poisons: taxine and potassium cyanide

Agatha Christie worked as a pharmacist during the first and second world wars, and therefore had considerable knowledge of drugs and poisons. In the story the murderer uses two different types of poison. The first was taxine, which comes from the yew tree. Yew is very common in Britain, especially in the formal gardens of rich people, such as the one at Yewtree Lodge, the home of the Fortescue family. The plant has thick dark green leaves which can easily be cut into different shapes, and gardeners often use it to make hedges and borders. All parts of the tree are extremely poisonous, including the red berries.

The second poison to be used in this story is potassium cyanide. When cyanide is put into liquid, it acts extremely quickly and death can happen in just a few seconds. At the time Agatha Christie was writing, it was normal for people to keep a form of cyanide in the garden shed to put on wasps' nests to kill them all quickly. Now, it is against the law to possess such poisons.

毒药：紫杉碱和氰化钾

阿加莎·克里斯蒂在第一次和第二次世界大战期间做过药剂师，所以具备相当的有关药品和毒药的知识。本书中罪犯使用了两种毒药，第一种是紫杉碱，来自紫杉树。紫杉在英国十分常见，尤其是在富翁的规则式庭园中，例如 Fortescue 家的居所紫杉公馆中的花园。这种植物的叶片厚实，呈绿色，可以轻易地切割为各种形状，于是园丁经常将其修剪为树篱和花坛。此种树的各部分均有剧毒，包括红色浆果。

故事中使用的第二种毒药是氰化钾。氰化物放入液体后，见效极其迅速，仅需几秒钟便可夺走人的性命。在阿加莎·克里斯蒂写作的时代，人们通常会在花园的工具棚中保存一些氰化物，用于快速消灭黄蜂的巢穴。如今存有这种毒药则是违法的。

The British class system

At the time when *A Pocket Full of Rye* was written in 1953, Britain still had a distinct class system with rules that everybody knew and followed, although the Second World War had done a lot to make these rules more relaxed. The *upper classes* owned land, had a lot of power and did not usually work for a living unless they were involved in politics, diplomacy or the military as very senior officers.

The *middle classes* were educated people who had to work for a living — they had professions in the law, medicine, education, the Church or, like Rex Fortescue, were in business, dealing with stocks and shares, investments and sometimes riskier projects. Sometimes businessmen like Rex Fortescue made a lot of money very quickly, and tried to behave in the same way that the upper classes did, creating a new social class, called the *nouveaux riches* or newly rich. Agatha Christie suggested throughout *A Pocket Full of Rye* that the Fortescue's belonged to this new class: Yewtree Lodge is described as being decorated expensively, but without taste; Adele has a very expensive sports car, the Rolls Bentley, which previously only the aristocratic upper class could afford — she also has a fake antique desk; Miss Marple is surprised when she meets Patricia because she obviously comes from a different (upper) class and had been married to a Lord.

The *working classes* had limited education, leaving school at the age of 14. Many worked in the houses of the wealthy like the Fortescues and there were several servants. Some lived in the house, some lived nearby. Servants included a butler — Crump; and housekeeper — Miss Dove; who were both in charge of the other servants: a cook — Mrs Crump; a housemaid who would do the rough cleaning; and a parlourmaid, too — Gladys, and there would usually be a gardener. Miss Marple was a kind woman who liked to help people. She found girls who were orphans or homeless and trained them to be parlourmaids, like Gladys, or other household servants.

英国的阶级系统

《黑麦奇案》写作于1953年，当时的英国仍保留着分明的阶级系统，设有各种公众均应知晓并遵守的规则，但第二次世界大战极大地影响了这些规则的执行。上层阶级拥有土地和权力，通常情况下不必为生计而工作，除非是在政治、外交或军事领域担任高级官员。

中产阶级的成员受过教育，必须为生计而奔波——就职于法律、医药、教育行业或教会，或者是像Rex Fortescue那样经商，与股票、债券和各类投资打交道，有时还会涉及风险更大的项目。像Rex Fortescue这样的商人偶尔会快速致富，并试图过上层阶级的生活，这样一来就创造了一个新的社会阶级，称为"暴发户"(nouveaux riches)。阿加莎·克里斯蒂通过《黑麦奇案》指明Fortescue家就属于这个新阶级：紫杉公馆富丽堂皇，但缺乏品味；Adele拥有劳斯莱斯-宾利这种原来只有上层贵族才负担得起的豪华跑车，但古董书桌却是冒牌货；Marple小姐遇到Patricia时吃了一惊，因为她显然来自不同（上层）阶级，曾嫁给贵族。

工人阶级受教育的程度有限，14岁时便会终止学业。很多人在Fortescue家这样的富贵人家中工作，此类人家大多雇有多名佣人。有些佣人住在富人家里，有些则住在附近。佣人中包括管家——Crump；女管家——Dove小姐；这二人是全体仆人的主管；厨师——Crump夫人；做清洁等脏活儿的女佣；以及用餐女侍——Gladys，通常还会有园丁。Marple小姐心地善良，乐于助人。她会去寻找孤儿或流浪儿，将其训练为像Gladys一样的用餐女侍或其他类别的家庭佣工。

The Cold War

The Cold War was a period of conflict and tension lasting approximately forty years. It was between mainly the USSR, which was communist, and the Western world, led by the USA which was capitalist. The USA's aim was to stop the spread of communism after the end of the Second World War. Anybody who was even suspected of having communist ideals was viewed with great suspicion. The fact that Elaine Fortescue wanted to marry a man who had 'communist ideas' was totally unacceptable to her family and that's why her father, Rex, threatened to stop supporting her if she married him.

冷战

冷战是充满了冲突和紧张的一段时期,持续了大约40年。对立的双方是以苏联为首的共产主义阵营和以美国为首的资本主义阵营。美国的目标是在第二次世界大战结束后阻止共产主义的扩张。即便是被怀疑怀有共产主义理想的人也会被视为具有重大嫌疑。Elaine Fortescue 想要嫁给一名拥有"共产主义理想"者的念头对她的家人来说是完全不能接受的,正因如此,她的父亲 Rex 才会威胁说如果她真嫁给他的话就会停止资助。

Truth drugs

When this story was written, there was considerable interest in a new kind of drug which would make people tell the truth. The newspapers printed stories about how both the Russian and

American governments had caught spies by giving them 'truth drugs'.

诱供药剂
在本书写就的年代,这种能够令人吐露真相的新型药物很能引起人们的兴趣。报纸上会刊登苏联和美国利用"诱供药剂"捕获双方间谍的新闻。

Wills and inheritance
A will is a legal document that describes how the money and property that someone leaves when they die is to be distributed to relatives and other people. Servants sometimes received a sum of money in a will. It was very unusual for a person with a fortune not to state where they wanted their money to go. It was therefore of great importance to the children and relatives of a rich person to know the details of their will. Wills were usually made in a solicitor's office but not always. To be legal, the signing of the will had to be witnessed, i.e. seen, by two people (usually not relatives) who knew the person writing the will.

遗嘱和遗产
遗嘱是一种法律文件,用来规定死者留下的钱财和财产如何分配给亲属和其他人。佣人偶尔也会通过遗嘱获得一笔钱财。对于财产可观者而言,不说明财产分配的情况非常少见。因此对于富翁的子女和亲属而言,搞清楚遗嘱的细节十分重要。遗嘱通常在律师事务所起草,但也有例外。为了使遗嘱拥有法律效力,遗嘱签字时必须有见证人,即两名(通常不为亲属)认识签字者的人在旁观看。

Holiday camps

In the years after the Second World War holiday camps became very popular. Until then, many working class people never had holidays. These camps weren't expensive; you paid a fixed amount for accommodation, food and entertainment and working class people like the parlourmaid Gladys in the story could afford a week's holiday. Holiday camps were not uncomfortable: there was plenty of food, they were warm, and there was endless hot water for baths — still a luxury for many British people at that time. There was always a lot of things for people to do, even when it rained non-stop for a whole week. They played sports and games, watched comedians, listened to live music and danced.

度假村

度假村在第二次世界大战结束后流行起来。在那以前,很多工人阶级从未有过假期。这些度假村的开销不高,只需支付固定的住宿、餐饮和娱乐费用,本书中像 Gladys 那样的用餐女侍也可以去享受为期一周的假期。度假村的生活条件良好:食物充足,气候温和,还有全天的洗澡热水——这对当时的很多英国人来说仍是一种奢侈。人们可干的事情总是很多,即便是在下了整整一周雨的情况下。他们可以进行体育活动、玩游戏、观看喜剧演出、聆听现场音乐演出并翩翩起舞。

Nursery rhymes

These are songs or poems for young children, often with actions added to them to make them more enjoyable and fun. Many of them are hundreds of years old, but these are mostly forgotten now. *A Pocket Full Of Rye* gets its name from a nursery rhyme called *Sing a Song of Sixpence*.

儿歌

这是为小孩子所作的歌曲或诗歌,通常会加入动作,使其更加好玩、有趣。不少儿歌已经有数百年的历史,但如今大多已被人遗忘。《黑麦奇案》的书名便是来自一首叫做"唱一首六便士的歌"(Sing a Song of Sixpence)的儿歌。

阿加莎·克里斯蒂经典侦探作品集

怪屋(Crooked House)

密码(N or M?)

魔手(The Moving Finger)

地狱之旅(Destination Unknown)

古屋疑云(Peril at End House)

借镜杀人(They Do It with Mirrors)

罗杰疑案(The Murder of Roger Ackroyd)

寓所谜案(The Murder at the Vicarage)

云中奇案(Death in the Clouds)

死亡约会(Appointment with Death)

葬礼之后(After the Funeral)

鸽群中的猫(Cat among the Pigeons)

命案目睹记(4.50 from Paddington)

闪光的氰化物(Sparkling Cyanide)

穿棕色套装的人(The Man in the Brown Suit)

国际学舍谋杀案(Hickory Dickory Dock)

斯泰尔斯庄园奇案(The Mysterious Affair at Styles)

黑麦奇案(A Pocket Full of Rye)

弄假成真(Dead Man's Folly)

书房命案(The Body in the Library)

悬崖上的谋杀案(Why Didn't They Ask Evans)

东方快车谋杀案(Murder on the Orient Express)

尼罗河上的惨案(Deadth on the Nile)

控方证人及其他(The Witness for the Prosecution and Other Stories)

图书在版编目(CIP)数据

黑麦奇案:英文/(英)阿加莎·克里斯蒂著.—北京:商务印书馆,2019
(阿加莎·克里斯蒂经典侦探作品集)
ISBN 978-7-100-15920-3

Ⅰ.①黑… Ⅱ.①阿… Ⅲ.①英语—语言读物②侦探小说—英国—现代 Ⅳ.①H319.4:I

中国版本图书馆 CIP 数据核字(2018)第 044244 号

权利保留,侵权必究。

阿加莎·克里斯蒂经典侦探作品集

黑麦奇案

〔英〕阿加莎·克里斯蒂 著

商 务 印 书 馆 出 版
(北京王府井大街36号 邮政编码100710)
商 务 印 书 馆 发 行
北 京 冠 中 印 刷 厂 印 刷
ISBN 978-7-100-15920-3

2019年7月第1版	开本 850×1168 1/32
2019年7月北京第1次印刷	印张 4⅜

定价:31.80元